AF662402

Updated

Knowledge Lighthouse

A SKILL-BASED COURSE ON GENERAL KNOWLEDGE

7

Name : ....

Grade: ....   Section : ....

India cultivates a diverse range of crops, including staples like rice, wheat, and pulses, as well as cash crops like cotton, tea, and spices. Draw the crops on the states where they are grown.

Seema Chari • Kunal Savarkar

HarperCollins*Publishers*

Publishing operations in 17 countries and 120+ imprints globally

William Collins' dream of knowledge for all began with the publication of his first book in 1819. A self-educated mill worker, he not only enriched millions of lives, but also founded a flourishing publishing house. Today, staying true to this spirit, Collins books are packed with inspiration, innovation and practical expertise. They place you at the centre of a world of possibility and give you exactly what you need to explore it.

Published by Collins Learning
An imprint of HarperCollins*Publishers* India
Building No. 10, Tower A, 4th Floor, DLF Cyber City, Gurugram, Haryana 122002, India

First edition: 2025
Reprint: 10 9 8 7 6 5 4 3 2 1
ISBN: 978-93-6213-388-5

Artwork, typesetting and layout by **GNZE Interactions**
Printed and bound in India by Thomson Press India Ltd

ACKNOWLEDGEMENTS

Cover and title page images: Anastasiia Ovsiannykova

Inside: Icons: Hiranmay Baidya, LvNL, cienpies, KaanC; **3:** impulse50; **4:** Natalia Darmoroz, impulse50; **5:** Natalia Darmoroz; **6:** Natalia Darmoroz, impulse50; **8:** Natalia Darmoroz, impulse50; **9:** MediaProduction; **10:** hmproudlove, Tuul & Bruno Morandi, RNMitra, Â©Daniela White Images, Imagery is, Marina Denisenko; **11:** Peter Chadwick LRPS, clickhere, sbossert, japatino, Martin Wahlborg, rutin55; **12:** ahireajay@gmail.com, vm2002; **13:** Noah Seelam, Nick Williams, CR Shelare, Amith Nag Photography; **14:** RobsonDuarte; **15:** avdeev007, Posnov, Michele D'Amico supersky77; **16:** arthobbit; **17:** Antonio Ribeiro, Paul Marotta, Stefan Cristian Cioata; **18:** Portra, andreonegin, RYosha; **19:** Emil von Maltitz, alpinetrail, guenterguni, mbbirdy, HomoCosmicos; **20:** yongyuan, tnakano, DigiPub; **21:** Fuse, Ultra.f, Aleaimage, GCShutter, Daqiao Photography; **22:** Michele Westmorland, olshole, Robert Pavsic; **24:** CatLane, abalcazar, CTRPhotos, Spinel_S, picture alliance; **25:** Noah Seelam, oksanaphoto, nilanewsom, NurPhoto, jayk7, ePhotocorp; **26:** Juanmonino, ailtonsza, Mantis17, NurPhoto; **27:** Cate Gillon, YT, Gabriel Bouys, **29:** SnowWhiteimages, Mike Egerton - PA Images; diegograndi; Kiran Chorge; RNMitra, Artie Photography (Artie Ng), Robbie Ross, Malcolm P Chapman, Prashant Kumar; **30:** EnginKorkmaz, Carlos Barquero Perez, Coast-to-Coast, Tassii; **31:** Danielrao, sauvik, vivalapenler, Sherman_Sham; **34:** GaryAlvis, J-Elgaard, LightFieldStudios; **35:** ottokalman, Henrik Sorensen, Ljupco; **36:** 200mm, Buena Vista Images, WWyloeck; **37:** Baron Reznik, Jason Edwards, bonchan, Kateryna Mashkevych; **38:** Â© Pascal Boegli, Westend61, mantaphoto, mkitina4; **39:** AlizadaStudios, mantaphoto; **40:** Ekspansio, fcafotodigital, evemilla, kyoshino, FotografiaBasica, xxmmxx, R.Tsubin, Flavio Coelho, Nenov, djmilic; **41:** republica, Turnervisual, yothinpi, robertsre, Jacky Parker Photography, Simon McGill; **42:** ericmichaud, NATALIA KOLESNIKOVA, I C Rapoport / Contributor, Maica, ttatty, pbombaert; **43:** isoft, KingWu, Boris25, DuKai photographer, Grafissimo; **44:** aeduard, jayk7, Nick Brundle Photography; **45:** Dorling Kindersley, Phototreat, Vincenzo De Palo Photo, Dion Lefeldt Rezaei; **46:** Davies, pixhook, Satirus; **47:** brlozier, JONATHAN NACKSTRAND; **48:** Bill Oxford; **49:** Bloomberg, Bettmann / Contributor, Bettmann, Dea Picture Library, Keystone; **50:** Coldimages, VanWyckExpress, freebilly, focusphotoart, Neha Gupta; **51:** Andrew_ Howe, ElementalImaging, wrangel, EcoPic, Rakesh C A; **52:** Science & Society Picture Library; **53:** Nigel Killeen, IndiaPictures, Hindustan Times, Michel Renaudeau; **54:** ImagineGolf, Photo and Co, Thomas Barwick, Mikhail Druzhinin / EyeEm; **55:** Hindustan Times, YinYang, George Pachantouris, Brian Bumby, travellinglight, Jana Kriz; **56:** Strdel, Carl Court, Sujit Jaiswal, Hindustan Times, Anthony Wallace; **57:** Jewel Samad, The Sydney Morning Herald, NicolÃ² Campo, Jam Media; **58:** Michael Ochs Archives, CBS Photo Archive, QAI Publishing; **59:** StockImages_AT, Sunset Boulevard, Kyodo News; **60:** Caspar Benson, Aj_OP, stockdevil, nanami_o; **61:** Pornchai Kittiwongsakul, J.W.Alker; **63:** Photographer Kris KrÃ¼g, Erin Donalson; **64:** The India Today Group, IndiaPictures, STRDEL, Bettmann; **65:** The India Today Group, IndiaPictures; **66:** Pascal Le Segretain, Bettmann / Contributor, Hulton Deutsch, Cole Burston, Mario Tama; **67:** Sven Nackstrand, Chip Somodevilla, Pascal Le Segretain, Pascal Le Segretain, Derek Hudson, Vittoriano Rastelli; **68:** Ewen Charlton, DavorLovincic, zanskar, Kieran Stone, Louise Docker Sydney Australia, Damocean; **70:** IPGGutenbergUKLtd, zanskar, FangXiaNuo, RomanBabakin; **72:** Hindustan Times, AFP Contributor; **73:** Neil Mockford / Contributor, RichLegg, huronphoto, Zocha_K, xxmmxx, Floortje, Feifei Cui-Paoluzzo, portishead1; **74:** Rafael_Wiedenmeier, Valerie Baeriswyl, NurPhoto; **75:** Anadolu Agency, FABRICE COFFRINI, Pierre Crom, Rich Fury; **79:** Getty Images, Mail Today, Francesco Prandoni, NurPhoto, Matt Winkelmeyer, Bruce Glikas; **82:** fabriziogiordano23, IndiaImages, SoumenNath, CR Shelare, RBB, vinod kumar m, leodaphne; **83:** saiko3p, Ramesh Lalwani, siraanamwong, Satvik Shahapur, Punit Paranjpe, Anil Dave; **84:** Science & Society Picture Library; **85:** Keystone / Stringer, DSK / Staff, Encyclopaedia Britannica, Bettmann; **87:** AFP, Mail Today, Carl Court, Hindustan Times, Ben Stansall, Mint

SDG logo and icons: https://www.un.org/sustainabledevelopment/

The content of this publication has not been approved by the United Nations and does not reflect the views of the United Nations or its officials or Member States.

Browse the complete Collins catalogue at www.collins.in.
For any queries/feedback, please write to us at SCHOOLSUPPORT@harpercollins.co.in.

Preface

Like the universe, knowledge, too, is limitless. No matter how much we know, there is always more to know. In the 21st century, thanks to the leaps that technology has made and continues to make, we shall have to gather knowledge throughout our lives; so much so that we have coined a new portmanteau, to describe it: 'upskilling'.

Another novelty of the third millennium is how we access and absorb knowledge. Apart from human sources (family, teachers, friends), there are the online ones (website, social media). Yet, despite all this easy availability and accessibility, it is not always easy to distinguish between real and fake, relevant and redundant, significant and inconsequential.

Updated Knowledge Lighthouse is a series meant for GenZ, that is, learners born after Y2K. The series covers 'classic' general knowledge content for learners of grades 1 to 8, but lays special emphasis on skills —learning skills, literacy skills and life skills— as well as knowledge gleaned from new learnings of the past few years, from COVID-19 to sustainability, from data science to global issues in an ever-shifting, ever-ephemeral, post-information world. All the new chapters, although dealing with topics of great gravity, are presented in an age-appropriate and friendly manner so as to kindle interest and lay the foundation for more in-depth learning.

A critical component of the Updated Knowledge Lighthouse books is the India content, wherein our country in all its complexity and diversity is presented through colourful, simple and exciting tasks, plus brand-new features such as state-focus, city-focus and visit-a-monument.

A particularly career-friendly inclusion in the Updated Knowledge Lighthouse series is Science, technology, engineering and mathematics (STEM), the disciplines of the future, and new global issues, presented under World Today. We hope to lighten these subjects for students, by adding a little sprinkle of trivia to them.

Sustainable development is one of the key phrases of this millennium, but what does it really mean for us, especially for children? The all-new Life on Land and Climate Action chapters not only sensitise learners but also encourage direct and immediate action.

In the Skills pages, the life skills section has tasks on safety and self-awareness. Connecting the dots is the foundation of knowledge and the series has chapters based on Higher Order Thinking Skills (HOTS) and critical thinking to train young minds to see patterns, learn to eliminate or choose details and observe better.

Become a Champion Quizzer

Updated Knowledge Lighthouse encourages all learners to be curious and explore the world around them. Those who observe and absorb all the time, learn from everyone and everything; they are the ones who become quizzers. Here are six rules that will help you become a champion quizzer.

1. Be curious—look around you, see everything, read everything.
2. Listen to others.
3. Seek out new experiences.
4. Learn to link events and people.
5. Do your own research and learn to spot fake news.
6. Remember, no matter how much you know, there is much more that you have yet to learn.

Now, go for it! We are sure that this series will expose a whole new generation of learners to the fun universe of general knowledge and enhance their love for learning and discovery.

~ Seema Chari and Kunal Savarkar

In this series ...

Updated Knowledge Lighthouse tasks are thematic and linear with visual, verbal, and strategic inputs to help students solve them and acquire knowledge through a wide range of subjects and themes.

World Around Us tasks take the learners on an exciting journey across the world.

Natural World section uncovers the magical realm of plants, animals and birds.

Sustainable Development Goals sensitises learners towards sustainable development of the planet.

India Focus tasks are created to evoke a sense of wonder and pride in our nation.

Art and Entertainment tasks celebrate artists, artworks, paintings, movies, awards and achievements.

Sports section provides rules and records related to different sports.

Language and Literature tasks present vocabulary and etymology in a fun way.

Word Today highlights the importance of understanding and addressing global challenges together.

Whiz Fact is a spin-off fact about each topic or theme.

STEM highlights some scientific achievements and provides facts for others.

Whiz Quiz are fun activities that encourage self-learning.

21st Century Skills

21st century skills are necessary to succeed in the Age of Information. These skills are divided into three main sets, namely, learning skills, literacy skills and life skills.

Learning Skills

- Critical Thinking and HOTS
- Creativity
- Collaboration
- Communication

6 Word Combinations

Learning Skills

A large travelling bag made of stiff leather that opened into two equal parts was called a portmanteau. Today, words made by combining the sounds and meanings of two different words are called portmanteau words. For example, brunch is a combination of breakfast and lunch.

Fill in the blanks to make these word sums about portmanteau words true.

	Word + Word =	Portmanteau Word
1	Haggle + Tussle =	....
2	.... + Complex =	Cineplex
3	Spoon + ... =	Spork
4	Smoke + Fog =	....
5	Lion + ... =	Liger
6	Emotion + Icon =	....

Literacy Skills

- Technology
- Information
- Media
- Financial Literacy
- Data Handling

16 Etiquette on the Internet

Literacy Skills

We follow specific rules of behaviour at home, at school and in the park. We also need to follow etiquette on the Internet.

Match the items in Column A with those in Column B to show you know the rules.

Column A	Column B
1 Flaming	a only in your personal chat. Do not use them for formal communication.
2 Spam	b is considered the same as shouting in real life. Do not do it.
3 Cyberbullying	c is an unsolicited, often commercial, message sent as a mass email. Do not disturb people by sending such messages.
4 Do not use acronyms	d and do not share their personal details or forward their messages unless you have their express permission to do so.
5 Respect people's time and bandwidth	e is the act of posting or sending offensive messages over any electronic medium. The offence is punishable by law.

Life Skills

- Problem-solving
- Self-awareness
- Safety
- Social Skills

8 Fire Safety

Life Skills

Read the following statements on fire safety. Draw ☺ for true and ☹ for false.

1. If the school's fire alarm starts ringing, you should continue with whatever you were doing because the principal is looking after the problem.
2. While escaping from a fire in a closed building, you should stay low. This way, you will avoid breathing in smoke as it tends to concentrate closer to the ceiling because hot air rises up.
3. If a mixer or toaster malfunctions and catches fire, you can use baking soda to control and extinguish the fire.
4. If you smell gas in the kitchen, you should ensure that stove knobs are in the off position and then

Detailed Contents

India Focus

- Travelling in South India
- Beaches of India
- Mahabalipuram
- Renowned Indian Statues
- Cash Crops of India
- The Indian Railways
- Northeast India Stars
- Tiger Conservation in India
- Indian Vocalists
- Indian Directors
- Roads and Highways in India
- Indian Diaspora
- UNESCO World Heritage Sites in India
- Insignia of the Indian Army

Sports

- Commonwealth Games
- Sporting Terms
- Kick-off Time!

Sustainable Development Goals

- Global Warming
- Environmentally Conscious Tourism

Learning Skills

- Word Combinations
- Countries Working Together
- Importing Words

Literacy Skills

- Etiquette on the Internet
- Inventors as Nouns
- Newspapers of India
- How Banks Work

Life Skills

- Fire Safety
- Scuba Diving

Contents

Language and Literature

1 Words of Indian Origin

The English language has many words of Indian origin.

Use the clues given below to locate such English words in the grid.

F	G	U	R	Y	T	E	R	I	C
E	V	M	B	M	O	D	C	G	H
P	D	A	C	O	I	T	K	G	E
B	U	N	G	A	L	O	W	F	E
J	U	G	G	E	R	N	A	U	T
A	D	O	U	O	R	T	S	E	A
S	C	H	O	L	T	E	A	R	H
M	A	H	O	U	T	U	T	S	H
F	S	Z	E	B	A	N	G	L	E
R	H	E	D	A	C	O	I	T	D

1. This word is derived from the Hindi word *bangla*, referring to Bengali-style houses.
2. This word is derived from the Tamil word *kasu* meaning 'money'.
3. This word comes from the Hindi word *daka* for robbery and refers to a member of a band of armed robbers.
4. This fruit takes its name from the Tamil word *maangai* which refers to its unripe form.
5. This word means one who takes care of elephants. It is derived from the Sanskrit word *mahāvat* meaning 'high official'.
6. This word comes from Jagannath, a deity worshipped in Puri, Odisha and it means an unstoppable force. It can also refer to a large, heavy vehicle.
7. This word comes from the Hindi word *bangli* or glass bracelet and refers to a rigid ornamental band worn around the wrist.
8. This word comes from the Sanskrit word *chitaka* meaning speckled and refers to the spotted big cat that is the fastest mammal on land.

Whiz fact

Every year, new words of Indian origin are added to English dictionaries. For instance, the Collins Dictionary lists the words *badmash*, *bhelpuri* and *churidar*.

2 National Trees

Along with national animals, birds and emblems, many countries also have national trees.

Fill the same letter in all the blanks of a clue to find the name of the national tree of each country.

1 INDI ..... N B ..... NY ..... N – India's national tree has roots coming down from the tree parallel to the tree trunk.

2 SUG ..... P ..... NE – The Japanese Red Cedar is a huge evergreen tree and considered sacred. The oldest such tree is between 2170 and 7200 years old and is still alive!

3 FRANG ..... PAN ..... – Also called plumeria, this tree with scented flowers is native to warm, tropical regions and is the national tree of Laos.

4 B ..... OB ..... B – The national tree of Madagascar grows in dry regions. Its trunk holds large quantities of water and it is leafless most of the year, so it looks as if its roots are sticking up in the air.

5 R ..... YAL ..... AK – The national tree of the United Kingdom is the one within which Charles II of England hid to escape his enemies after the Battle of Worcester in 1651.

6 ..... EO ..... AR – This large evergreen coniferous tree has needle-shaped leaves, level branches and a cone-shaped crown at the top. It is the national tree of Pakistan.

7 WI .... OW – The national tree of Ukraine, this tree grows in moist soil in cold and temperate regions of the Northern Hemisphere.

8 COR ..... OA ..... – Portugal's national tree makes up 23% of the country's forest area and supports its main industry. This species of tree has been protected by law since the 13th century.

9 RHO ..... O ..... EN ..... RON – A woody plant found mainly in Asia, Nepal's national tree has brightly coloured flowers that bloom from late winter to early summer.

10 S ..... LVER B ..... RCH – This thin-leaved deciduous national tree of Finland has hardwood that can be shaped with power tools. Its sap is used to make a traditional drink and also birch syrup to pour onto pancakes and waffles.

11 SIBE ..... IAN FI ..... . – Russia's national tree is coniferous and evergreen. Its wood is used in construction, furniture and wood pulp, and its leaves give essential oils used for aromatherapy and perfume.

12 SILVE ..... FE ..... N – This medium-sized tree fern is native to New Zealand. The distinctive colouration of the leaves makes the plant useful for laying along tracks for night walking.

Whiz fact

The Manchineel tree, native to Florida, is considered the most poisonous tree in the world. It causes painful blisters if you stand under it during rain. Its smoke and sawdust burn skin, eyes and lungs, and its fruit can be fatal if eaten.

India Focus

3 Travelling in South India

South India consists of five states—Tamil Nadu, Kerala, Karnataka, Andhra Pradesh and Telangana—and the union territory of Puducherry.

Find the answers to the blanks in each statement using the help box.

1. This city in Karnataka is famous for its glittering royal heritage, magnificent monuments and delicious ghee-based sweet named after it. The sweet is called .... pak.

2. ...., earlier called Trivandrum, is called the 'beach city of Kerala'.

3. .... in Tamil Nadu is called the 'Manchester of South India' because of its extensive textile industry, which is fed by the surrounding cotton fields.

4. A port city of Andhra Pradesh, ... is famous for its shipyard, steel plant, beaches and the Araku Valley, a popular tourist destination.

5. A UNESCO World Heritage site in Karnataka, ... lies within the ruins of the ancient temple complexes of the Vijayanagara Empire.

6. Earlier called Calicut, ... was once a famous cotton-weaving centre and gave its name to calico cloth.

7. .... is the capital of Telangana and is currently being shared by Andhra Pradesh.

8 An important industrial and educational hub in Tamil Nadu, ... is well-known for the Meenakshi Amman Temple.

9 Famous for its shrines, ... in Andhra Pradesh is best known for the renowned Sri Venkateswara Temple located at the top of the Tirumala Hills.

10 The capital city of Karnataka, ... is popularly known as the 'Silicon Valley of India'.

11 The city of .... in Telangana has a fort of the same name, the Ashok Sagar Lake and the Badapahad Dargah, one of the oldest Muslim pilgrimage centres.

12 Earlier known as Cochin, ... is a major port city and is known as the financial, commercial and industrial capital of Kerala.

13 The new capital of Andhra Pradesh is ....

14 .... is the second largest city in Telangana. The Thousand Pillar Temple situated on Hanamkonda hill is one of its most popular tourist destinations.

15 Most of the Great Living Chola Temples, which are UNESCO World Heritage Monuments, are located near .... in Tamil Nadu. It is also home to the Tanjore style of painting.

Help box

Amaravati	Thanjavur	Coimbatore	Tirupati	Mysore
Kochi	Madurai	Nizamabad	Warangal	Kozhikode
Hyderabad	Hampi	Thiruvananthapuram	Bengaluru	Visakhapatnam

Whiz fact

The union territory of Puducherry comprises four separate enclaves—two on the western coast and two on the eastern coast of India.

4 Good Books

Here are the names of some of the famous books, but one letter in the title has been misspelled. *The misspelled word has been underlined. Use the clue to change the word and find the correct title.*

1. The Book Chief – a girl steals books
2. Diary of a Wimpy Lid – a child who narrates the problems of his life
3. James and the Giant Beach – a child makes friends with many insects that live in a fruit
4. Twenty Thousand Leagues Under the Tea – an ocean adventure
5. The Bungle Book – a story of a boy brought up by a wolf pack
6. Charlotte's Wet – a story of friendship between a pig and a spider
7. The Thousand and One Tights – a series of Middle eastern folk tales that are told over many years as bedtime stories by a queen to a king
8. Aesop's Tables – animal stories with a moral at the end
9. The Secret Warden – a spoilt girl is curious about a mysterious garden when she is sent to live with her uncle
10. Anne of Green Cables – a girl called Anne helps out on a farm
11. A Wrinkle in Tame – a girl, her brother and a friend travel through time to rescue her father from a distant planet
12. Slack Beauty – a story about the life of a black horse, told as if the horse were writing it

Whiz fact

The *Epic of Gilgamesh*, written nearly 4000 years ago, is the oldest written story. It is originally written on 12 clay tablets in the earliest known script called cuneiform.

Natural World

5 Lakes of the World

Lakes are bodies of freshwater enclosed by land on all sides.

Read the sentences and find the answers in the grid to fill in the blanks. The first letter of each answer is shown in blue in the word grid to help you. Words can move in any direction in the grid.

1. The deepest lake in the world, Lake .... is located in Russia and provides 20% of the world's freshwater.
2. The second-deepest lake in the world, Lake .... forms a boundary between Tanzania and Congo.

3. The largest of the five Great Lakes of North America, Lake .... is bordered by the US states of Michigan, Wisconsin and Minnesota, and the Canadian province of Ontario.

V	A	S	D	F	A	E	I	B	T
I	W	A	L	A	M	U	O	A	M
C	E	I	U	A	W	P	Q	I	F
T	A	N	G	A	N	Y	I	K	A
O	X	T	V	D	W	U	J	A	G
R	O	I	R	E	P	U	S	L	L
I	L	O	C	H	N	E	S	S	E
A	K	P	B	J	M	A	G	K	Z

4. With the largest volume of freshwater in Great Britain, Scotland's .... is said to be inhabited by a folkloric monster.
5. The largest reservoir feeding the Nile river, Lake ...., named after a former Queen of England, is one of Africa's Great Lakes.
6. Lake ...., also called Lake Nyasa, is another of Africa's Great Lakes. The first European to report its existence was a Portuguese named Caspar Boccaro in 1616.

Whiz fact

The Caspian Sea, bordered by Russia, Iran, Azerbaijan, Kazakhstan and Turkmenistan, is the world's largest lake. It was named after the Kaspi people who lived on its southwestern shores.

Learning Skills

6 Word Combinations

A large travelling bag made of stiff leather that opened into two equal parts was called a portmanteau. Today, words made by combining the sounds and meanings of two different words are called portmanteau words. For example, brunch is a combination of breakfast and lunch.

CRITICAL THINKING

Fill in the blanks to make these word sums about portmanteau words true.

Word + Word =	Portmanteau Word
1 Haggle + Tussle =	....
2 .... + Complex =	Cineplex
3 Spoon + ... =	Spork
4 Smoke + Fog =	....
5 Lion + ... =	Liger
6 Emotion + Icon =	....
7 Gigantic + ... =	Ginormous
8 .... + Fabulous =	Fantabulous
9 Motor + ... =	Motel
10 International + Network =	....

Whiz quiz

A portmanteau can equally be applied to proper nouns. An example is Brexit, which neatly describes the exit of Britain from the European Union. Some spinoffs of this include Grexit and Exitalia. Can you guess which countries are referred to by these?

13 CLIMATE ACTION

Climate Action

7 Global Warming

Fill in the blanks using the help box to complete these statements about global warming.

1. The United Nations Conference on Environment and Development (UNCED) was held in .... in 1992, where more than 170 countries came to an agreement on climate change.

2. One of the results of global warming is the rise in sea level due to the melting of polar ice caps. Scientists believe that the island nation of .... is in danger of submerging about 80 years from now.

3. As a result of the Earth Summit, the ...., an international treaty, was signed in 1997 by over 150 countries, who agreed to reduce greenhouse gas emissions.

4. .... is a measure of the total amount of carbon dioxide produced by the daily activities of a person or an organisation.

5. The environmentalist and former Vice President of the US, Al Gore, was awarded the Nobel Prize for Peace in 2007 along with IPCC, a scientific intergovernmental body of the ....

6. The Oscar winning documentary, ... was on Al Gore's campaign to educate citizens about global warming.

7. The .... is an international treaty to protect the ozone layer by phasing out the production of ozone-depleting substances.

Help box

Kyoto Protocol	Rio de Janeiro	Carbon Footprint	An Inconvenient Truth
United Nation	Montreal protocol	Maldives	

Whiz fact

Global warming and climate change are sometimes used interchangeably, but they are not the same thing. The former is the gradual increase of the earth's temperature, while the latter represents changes in weather patterns and crop growing seasons. Both are aggravated by the overuse of fossil fuels.

Life Skills

8 Fire Safety

Read the following statements on fire safety. Draw 🙂 for true and 🙁 for false.

1. If the school's fire alarm starts ringing, you should continue with whatever you were doing because the principal is looking after the problem.

2. While escaping from a fire in a closed building, you should stay low. This way, you will avoid breathing in smoke as it tends to concentrate closer to the ceiling because hot air rises up.

3. If a mixer or toaster malfunctions and catches fire, you can use baking soda to control and extinguish the fire.

4. If you smell gas in the kitchen, you should ensure that stove knobs are in the off position and then open all the doors and windows.

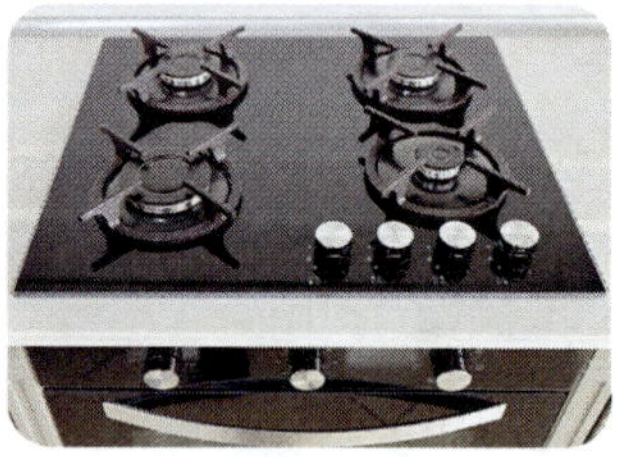

5. While leaving a room which is on fire, you should close the door behind you because this will ensure that the smoke, fire and heat do not spread to other areas.

6. While conducting experiments in a laboratory, you should use chemicals containing alcohol near a bunsen burner.

Whiz fact

A fire can occur if three components are present at the same time: heat, oxygen and fuel. If the levels of these components stay stable, a fire will only grow bigger with every minute.

9 Waterfalls

A waterfall is a vertical drop or a series of steep falls in the course of a stream, a river or other waterbodies. Waterfalls often form in the upper stages of a river where water erodes soft rock more quickly than hard rock.

Use the clues and the help box to find the names of the world's most famous waterfalls.

1. .... Falls in Venezuela is the tallest or highest waterfall in the world, with water falling from a height of 979 metres, 15 times higher than the Niagara Falls.

2. .... Falls in Romania is unique in its beauty because of the way the water spreads and falls. It is located exactly on the 45th parallel North, at the halfway point between the Equator and the North Pole.

3. .... Falls was formed in the last ice age and is the largest waterfall in Switzerland and in Europe.

4. .... Falls in the Amazon rainforest in Guyana is the largest single drop waterfall in the world, with five times the volume of water compared to Niagara Falls and almost twice as high as Victoria Falls.

5. .... Falls in Iceland was once privately owned, but is now state-owned and part of the 'Golden Circle'.

6. .... Falls in Karnataka, is the highest waterfall in India, falling from a height of 455 metres. It has the only permanent rainforest research station in India.

7. .... Falls in Zambia is the largest waterfall in the world considering its height and width. It is considered one of the Seven Natural Wonders of the World. The spray from this waterfall can be seen from a distance of 50 km.

Help box

Rhine | Bigar Cascade | Gullfoss | Kunchikal | Kaieteur | Angel | Victoria

Whiz fact

The ancient Romans created the Cascata delle Marmore (Marmore Falls) in Italy, having a total height of 165 metres (541 feet). This makes it the tallest man-made waterfall in the world.

World Around Us

10 A Trip to Japan

With over 6800 islands and around 1500 earthquakes a year, Japan occupies a unique place on Earth.

Read the sentences and find the answers in the grid to fill in the blanks. The first letter of each answer is shown in blue in the word grid to help you.

S	S	U	M	O	R	M	C	A	R	E	T	S	H
B	E	N	T	O	B	O	X	D	R	A	T	H	R
G	N	T	G	I	T	U	R	O	U	S	T	I	R
G	S	Z	S	H	I	N	K	A	N	S	E	N	S
T	E	T	H	R	Z	T	R	K	A	R	A	T	E
K	I	M	O	N	O	F	T	O	R	N	E	O	R
U	F	I	G	E	S	U	S	H	I	R	E	M	A
I	H	J	U	D	O	J	F	C	R	E	T	A	E
P	E	R	N	S	E	I	K	E	B	A	N	A	D

1 .... is the Japanese name for what we know as bullet trains.

2 ...., the highest mountain in Japan, is considered sacred.

3 .... refers to a Japanese meal that is packed in a special box.

4 .... was the title given to military commanders who more or less ruled Japan from 1192 to 1867.

5 .... is the art of Japanese flower arrangement.

6 .... is the traditional Japanese robe, earlier worn by both men and women, but nowadays, worn largely by women.

7 .... is the name given to a teacher or master of anything, not just martial arts.

8 .... is a type of Japanese food prepared with brown or white rice, raw seafood and seaweed.

9 .... is a religion followed by many Japanese people.

10 .... is the form of wrestling traditionally practised in Japan.

11 ...., which means 'the gentle way', is a modern Japanese martial art.

12 .... is an ancient Japanese martial art used for self-defence.

Whiz fact

The Japanese language often expresses complex or quirky thoughts considered difficult or impossible to express in other languages. One is 'sundoku', which means the tendency to compulsively buy books that one can or will never read. Do you know anybody who suffers from sundoku?

11 Scuba Diving

Life Skills

'Scuba' in scuba diving is actually an acronym. It stands for Self-Contained Underwater Breathing Apparatus. A diver uses SCUBA to breathe underwater.

Underline every third word in each sentence to put together the ten safety rules of scuba diving. Then, write them down in the space provided. One has been done for you.

1. Steam is never to be hold treated lightly your lest it breath damage the or skin of you your body may it could damage even cause your serious burns lungs.

   Never hold your breath or you may damage your lungs.

2. It is ascend a matter slowly of principle and that we safely should keep at an eye all towards safety times.

3. One of check the rules your behind safety gear is to and think ahead make so that sure one is you always prepared know for various how sorts of to situations that use may arise it.

4. Flying in never the face dive of caution beyond never did your anyone any qualification good level or it at your your own comfort risk time zone.

5. Plan to stay practise what physically you want fit to do to so that increase your muscles safety are prepared on for it dives.

6 Certainly you plan must visit your your near dive and dear and ones before dive you go your to reassure plan.

....

....

7 Start working use out only one when you third have met of a doctor your who will air certify that supply you are going fit to down, participate in another the activity third you are during going for the not doing return, so journey and morale of the the team final adversely and third is utterly as undesirable so a please keep safety in mind reserve.

....

....

8 Stay ready use to go the the moment buddy the supervisor system summons you unless so you you do not have impede others been who have properly also been trained looking forward to to this dive lovely opportunity alone.

....

....

9 Find a practise lonely spot vital and take skills time out to to meditate avoid so that injury you are and very calm accidents.

....

....

10 Smile and establish keep an positive upbeat mindset buoyancy this will at help you the at all surface. Times to this overcome the means blues you you may occasionally should feel and float you will easily also be when great company you for others reach in the the adventure team surface.

....

....

Whiz quiz

Scuba divers sometimes use wet suits and sometimes use dry suits while on dives. When would they wear either of the two?

Whiz fact

In *Finding Nemo,* the art team took scuba diving courses in oceanography, marine biology and other fields to understand the underwater world better!

Language and Literature

12 Harry Potter Quiz

The *Harry Potter* series started out as a children's fantasy but has become an enduring modern classic.

Take this quiz to find out how much you know about the world of the wizard with the scar on his forehead.

1. What object must be caught in order to end a Quidditch match? ....

2. What position does Ron Weasley play for the Gryffindor Quidditch team? ....

3. Which animal does Professor Moody change Draco Malfoy into? ....

4. Which monster lives in the Chamber of Secrets? ....

5. What spell is used to protect oneself from spells that are dangerous? ....

6. What does the Hogwarts motto *Draco dormiens nunquam titillandus* mean in English? ....

7. Which newspaper do the witches and wizards read? ....

8. What type of broom does Harry get from his godfather Sirius? ....

9. Hagrid had a boarhound. What was the dog's name? ....

10. Where does Mr Weasley work? ....

11. Who guards the entrance to the Gryffindor common room? ....

12. Which prison was Gellert Grindelwald sent to? ....

13. What did Dobby catch that set him free from the Malfoy family? ....

14. What is the name of Dumbledore's phoenix? ....

Whiz fact

J K Rowling, the author of the *Harry Potter* series, shares many things with her characters. She and Harry share a birthday, her favourite animal is an otter, which is Hermione's Patronus, and both she and Dumbledore like sherbet lemons.

World Around Us

13 Let's Visit Argentina!

Read the following statements and use the help box to fill in the blanks to learn some interesting facts about Argentina.

1. Ushuaia on the Argentine island of Tierra del Fuego is the world's .... city, with 57,000 residents.
2. One of the most popular dances in the world, the ...., originated in Buenos Aires, the capital of Argentina.
3. The .... in Argentina is the third-largest reserve of freshwater in the world and one of the few glaciers that is growing instead of shrinking.

4. .... in the Andes is the highest point in Argentina and outside Asia.
5. Argentina became the first country to use .... as a method of identification in 1891.

6. The ...., famed for its fur, is Argentina's most endangered animal.

7. The Argentinian soccer hero .... is arguably considered the world's best footballer.
8. Argentina has been the uninterrupted .... champion since 1949 and is the source of most of the world's top 10 .... (same word) matches today.

Help box

fingerprinting	chinchilla	polo	Mount Aconcagua	tango
southernmost	Lionel Messi	Perito Moreno		

Whiz fact

In Argentina, both adults and children travel home to take a *siesta* after their midday meal. A *siesta* is a short nap taken in the afternoon.

Art and Entertainment

14 Artistes Extraordinaires

Look at the works of some celebrated artists. Write the correct number in the boxes to match the artists's name and description of their work with what they created.

The Sistine Chapel ceiling ☐

Marilyn Monroe ☐

Goldfish ☐

The Son of Man ☐

Guernica ☐

Starry Night ☐

1. Vincent van Gogh was a Dutch painter who created breathtaking paintings of nature.
2. Pablo Picasso was a Spanish painter whose work has a lot of geometric shapes in it.
3. American artist Andy Warhol was a leading figure in the Pop Art movement. He is known for his vivid work of iconic American objects and celebrities.
4. Henri Matisse was a French artist whose subjects were simple, while his brushwork seemed wild. He used clashing colours.
5. Belgian artist René Magritte was a painter whose witty, thought-provoking paintings have a photographic quality.
6. One of the greatest painters and sculptors of the Italian Renaissance, Michelangelo's famous work depicts scenes from the Genesis.

Whiz fact

The Last Supper is a masterpiece by polymath, Leonardo da Vinci. It is painted on a wall of the dining hall in the Convent of Santa Maria delle Grazie in Milan, Italy.

Literacy Skills

15 Etiquette on the Internet

We follow specific rules of behaviour at home, at school and in the park. We also need to follow etiquette on the Internet.

Match the items in Column A with those in Column B to show you know the rules.

TECHNOLOGY

Column A	Column B
1 Flaming	a only in your personal chat. Do not use them for formal communication.
2 Spam	b is considered the same as shouting in real life. Do not do it.
3 Cyberbullying	c is an unsolicited, often commercial, message sent as a mass email. Do not disturb people by sending such messages.
4 Do not use acronyms	d and do not share their personal details or forward their messages unless you have their express permission to do so.
5 Respect people's time and bandwidth	e is the act of posting or sending offensive messages over any electronic medium. The offence is punishable by law.
6 Respect people's privacy	f is the use of social networks to harm or harass a person.
7 Use appropriate emoticons	g by not loading heavy attachments on a common forum.
8 Typing in all capital letters	h like LOL, ROFL, BRB, etc. People may not know what they stand for and they are not acceptable in formal communication.

Whiz Advice

If someone writes, posts or forwards something bad about you on the Internet, report it immediately to adults you trust.

India Focus

16 Mahabalipuram

Read this text about a UNESCO World Heritage Site in Tamil Nadu and choose the correct answer among the options given.

The seaside town of (1) Mamallapuram/Cholamandalam/Kanchipuram or Mahabalipuram in Tamil Nadu is world famous not only for its beautiful shoreline and sandy (2) beach/desert/hillock, but also for a collection of 400 monuments that date back to the 7th and 8th centuries CE. The word *Mamalla* means 'great wrestler'. The town lies about 60 kilometres south of Chennai on the (3) Malabar/Konkan/Coromandel Coast. The monuments were built by the (4) Pallava/Maurya/Chandela Dynasty. Let us read about some of the most renowned monuments.

'Descent of the (5) Himalayas/Shivalingam/Ganges', also called 'Arjuna's or Bhagiratha's Penance', is the largest open air rock relief in the world. Mahabalipuram is a collection of rathas or (6) boat/chariot/pillar-shaped temples, several mandapas or cave temples dedicated to gods as well as characters from Hindu mythology, such as from the (7) Mahabharata/Panchatantra/Dhammapada and the spectacular (8) hill/forest.

There are other sculptures, including rock animals like *Nandi* the (9) cow/tiger/bull, an elephant and lions, carved mainly out of granite. The complex miraculously survived the mighty (10) volcano/tsunami/cloudburst of December 2004, during which many more constructions were spotted under the sea. Archaeologists are now exploring these undersea wonders.

Whiz fact

Among the human marvels in Mahabalipuram is a miracle of nature: a huge semi-spherical boulder affectionately called Krishna's butter-ball precariously perched on a rocky slope. Many have tried to get the 250 ton boulder to roll down the hill, but it has remained stubbornly in place, drawing thousands of tourists every year!

Sports

17 Commonwealth Games

The Commonwealth Games is an international multi-sport event involving athletes from the Commonwealth of Nations.

Add 2 letter groups to find the answers to the blanks in each statement.

MALAY	ORIA
AUS	SIA
BOR	TRALIA
VICT	OBI
BIRMIN	STLE
THI	GHAM

1. The host city for the 2022 Commonwealth Games was ....
2. .... was the first Asian nation to host the Commonwealth Games in 1998.
3. Clyde, the first non-animal mascot of the 2014 Commonwealth Games held in Glasgow, was a ....
4. Athletes with a disability were first included in exhibition events at the 1994 Commonwealth Games in ...., British Columbia. At the 2002 Games, they were included as full members of their national teams.

5. ...., a koala with blue fur and unusual markings on his paws, was the official mascot of the 2018 Commonwealth Games held at Gold Coast, Australia.
6. .... has hosted the Commonwealth Games five times, the first time in 1938.

Whiz fact

The first Commonwealth Games held in 1930 was called the British Empire Games. The name was changed to British Empire and Commonwealth Games in 1954, to British Commonwealth Games in 1970 and finally to Commonwealth Games in 1978.

18 Social Movements of the 21st Century

World Today

As we mark the silver jubilee of this century, we can see that people of the twenty-first century are more vocal than ever before, and members of every community have increasingly found a public voice through mass movements. Some of these are triggered by immediate causes, while others have been simmering for a while before finding expression. Match these social movements with their description and write the name of the country in which they originated.

Name	Description	Country of origin
1 Jasmine Revolution/ Arab Spring 	a Led by social activist Anna Hazare, this 2011 movement saw protests across the country by citizens fighting against widespread corruption.	
2 Schools Strike for Climate 	b This 2011 movement led to people talking about economic inequality and corporate greed; and the impact of wealth on law-making in the world's richest country.	
3 Black Lives Matter 	c This short but successful 2010-11 people's agitation against dictatorship and corruption led to democratisation in this country in north Africa, and free and fair elections.	

Whiz fact

People don't always take to the streets to register protest or solidarity for a cause. Many practise 'internet activism' by signing petitions for or against some social or political ill, on sites like change.org, avaaz.org, getup.org.au. Passive signing or 'liking' of something serious may or may not lead to actual change and is sometimes referred to as 'slacktivism'.

4 MeToo 	d Its name refers to the peaceful protests in this Asian city in 2014, in reference to the umbrellas used for defence against tear gas and pepper spray used by police officers against protesters.	
5 Anti-Corruption Movement 	e Activist Tarana Burke sparked this movement in 2006. She wanted to break the silence surrounding sexual assault, rape and harassment, and empower women through empathy and strength in numbers.	
6 Nirbhaya Movement 	f Led by schoolgirl Greta Thunberg, this 2018-19 movement led top global student protests against the lack of action by governments and industry to reverse climate change.	
7 Occupy Wall Street 	g This countrywide mass movement followed the tragic 2012 case of Nirbhaya and led to a change in laws dealing with atrocities on women.	
8 Umbrella Movement 	h This campaign aims to end violence and systemic racism towards black people and other people of colour.	

Help box

USA, Hong Kong, Tunisia, India, Sweden, India, USA, USA

India Focus

19 Renowned Indian Statues

Solve the crossword to identify the cities in which each famous statue of India is located.

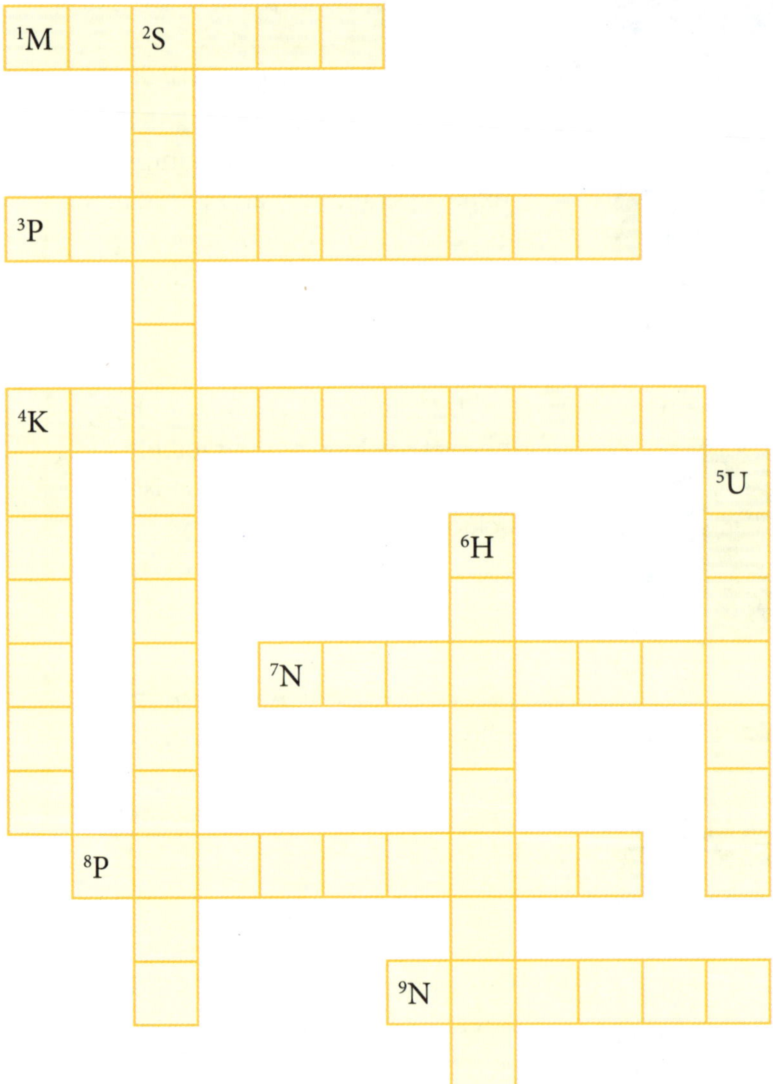

Across

1 This statue of Nandi the bull is located outside a temple in this Karnataka city. (6)

3 This statue of Chhatrapati Shivaji Maharaj on his horse is in this fort in Maharashtra. (10)

4 This statue of Tamil poet and philosopher Valluvar is in this very southerly Tamil Nadu town. (11)

7 This statue of Gandhiji leading freedom fighters is called Gyarah Murti. It is close to the Rashtrapati Bhavan in this megalopolis. (8)

8 This statue of V D Savarkar is at the Cellular Jail in the capital of the Andaman and Nicobar Islands. (4, 5)

9 This statue of Padmasambhava Guru Rinpoche is in this place in Sikkim. (6)

Down

2 This statue of Gomateshwara, also known as Bahubali, is in Karnataka in this area. (16)

4 This statue of Queen Victoria on her throne is in this huge city in West Bengal. (7)

5 The Maharana Pratap Memorial is in this lake city of Rajasthan. (7)

6 This statue of the Buddha is on an island in the Hussain Sagar Lake in this millennium city in Telangana. (9)

Whiz fact

The world's tallest statue is the Statue of Unity in Gujarat. It is 182 m tall and depicts the great freedom fighter, Sardar Vallabhbhai Patel. More recently, the Statue of Equality was sculpted and inaugurated in Hyderabad. At 216 feet, it is the third largest sitting statue in the world.

Art and Entertainment

20 Genres of Music

A music genre is a conventional category that identifies some pieces of music as belonging to a shared tradition or set of conventions.

Read the following statements and use the help box to identify various genres of music to fill in the blanks. The number of blank spaces is equal to the number of letters.

1. This genre of music originated in the southern United States in the early 1920s. It takes its roots from Appalachian folk music, Western music and blues.

   ....

2. Music incorporating elements of rhythm and blues and gospel music popularised by African Americans, this genre is characterised by an emphasis on vocals and an impassioned, improvised delivery.

   ....

3. This loud, aggressive style of rock music has loud, powerful-sounding songs and strong rhythms.

   ....

   ....

4. This genre of Christian music is a fervent style of evangelical religious singing developed from spirituals sung in Baptist and Pentecostal churches in the Southern United States.

   ....

5. This is structured music written in Europe during the years 1550 to 1900 following long-established principles.

   ....

6. This music originated from traditional culture, is typically of unknown authorship and is transmitted orally from generation to generation. The 20th century folk revival established this tradition as a genre. Today, folk singers write folk songs following the same style and tradition.

   ....

7 A style of popular music that originated in Jamaica in the late 1960s, it became the country's dominant music. By the 1970s, it had become an international style that was widely perceived as a voice of the oppressed.

....

8 Developed in the US by inner-city African Americans in the late 1970s, this genre of music consists of a stylized rhythmic music that commonly accompanies rapping, a rhythmic and rhyming speech that is chanted.

....

9 Invented in New Orleans, United States, in the late 19th and early 20th centuries, this genre combines African American music with European music.

....

10 Type of music with a rhythmic element, simple structure and themes, and catchy tunes and hooks, which is often "singles-based", that is, a single song, and mostly aimed at younger audiences such as teenagers.

....

11 This type of music encompasses diverse themes, makes extensive use of the amplified electric guitar and often has dissonant harmonies and greater aggression. It, therefore, appeals to more mature listeners.

....

Help box

Classical   Country   Folk   Pop   Gospel   Heavy Metal
Hip-hop   Rock   Jazz   Reggae   Soul

Whiz fact

In 1989, General Noriega, the dictatorial ruler of Panama, took refuge in the Vatican. For two days, the US military bombarded him 24 hours a day with songs from AC/DC such as 'Highway to Hell'. The ex-dictator surrendered!

World Around Us

21 Let's Visit Bhutan!

The kingdom of Bhutan is one of the most isolated nations in the world.

Use the help box to fill in the blanks to find out more about Bhutan.

1 The Bhutanese call their home '*Druk Yul*', which means .... because of the extremely powerful storms that constantly blow in from the Himalayas.

2 The official language of Bhutan is ....

3 The country's national sport is ....

4 Bhutan is the only country in the world to outlaw .... This has been in effect since 2004.

5 Bhutan's capital Thimphu is one of only two capital cities in the world without ....

6 Bhutan's national animal is a goat-antelope called the ....

7 .... is the country's official religion.

8 The .... National Park is the only park where the national animal, the national flower (the blue poppy), the national bird (raven) and the national tree (cypress) exist together in the same place.

9 Paro Taktsang or the ...., a small collection of buildings perched precariously on a cliff, is a renowned tourist spot in Bhutan.

10 .... has the only international airport of the country.

11 *Ema datshi* is a popular dish made with .... and cheese.

12 Women in Bhutan traditionally wear the *kira*, a long .... dress.

Help box

archery	ankle-length	takin	Tiger's Nest Monastery
chillies	Paro	Jigme Dorji	tobacco
Buddhism	traffic lights	Dzongkha	Land of Thunder Dragon

Whiz fact

Bhutan is the world's first carbon sink country, meaning it absorbs more carbon dioxide than it gives out. Its largest export is hydroelectric power, accounting for about half of all its exports.

Natural World

22 Glaciers of the World

Glaciers are formed when snow collects in huge quantities and, instead of melting, hardens into ice. A special feature of glaciers is that they are not static but move very slowly.

Use the help box to fill in two blanks for each answer, then fill in the acrostic with the names of prominent glaciers from around the world. When you read down the highlighted column, you will find the name of the world's largest glacier, which is located in Antarctica.

1 The Yulong glacier is on top of ....'s Yulong .... It has been retreating since the 1980s and scientists predict that it might be gone in in the next few years from now.

2 Vatnajökull in .... is one of Europe's largest glaciers and the largest in the country. It has several active .... beneath it.

3 The Jostedalsbreen is continental Europe's largest glacier. It is located in .... and covers more than 50% of the Jostedalsbreen .... Park.

4 Furtwängler is ....'s most famous glacier. It is situated on Mt .... Since climate change has melted most of its ice and no new ice has formed on it since the year 2000, this glacier might disappear by 2040.

5 ....'s Pasterze is the longest glacier in the eastern .... Global warming has resulted in its losing more than half its volume and it is retreating as much as 10–20 metres each year.

6 The Kutiah glacier in .... holds the record for the fastest movement. It moved more than 12 .... in three months in 1953.

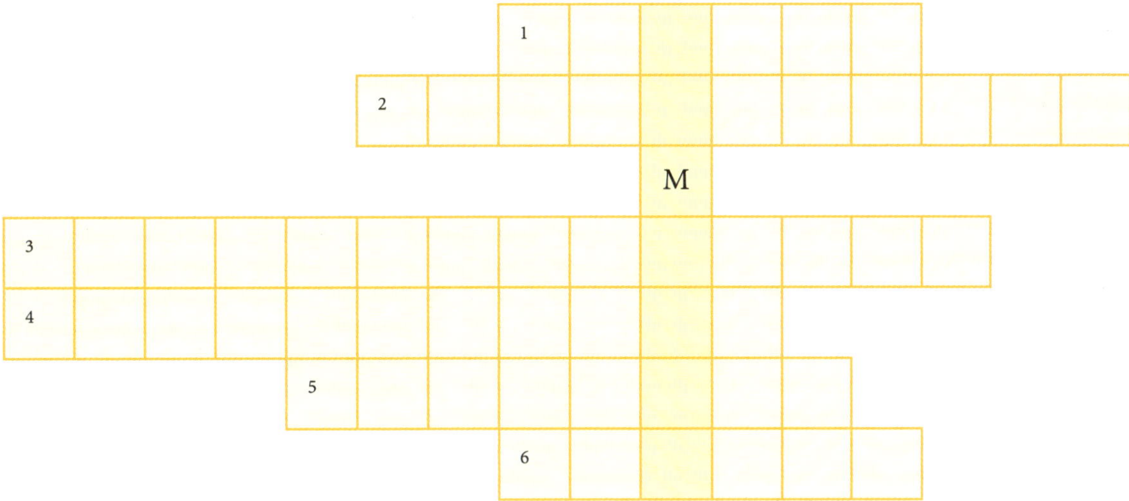

Help box

Africa, Kilimanjaro	Iceland, volcanoes	Pakistan, kilometres
Austria, Alps	China, mountain	Norway, National

Whiz quiz

People who study glaciers are called glaciologists. Can you guess who researches on the following?

1 oceans .... 2 earth .... 3 climate ....

Whiz fact

If all land ice melted, sea level would rise approximately 70 m worldwide. That's approximately 230 feet and would flood most coastal cities across the world!

India Focus

23 Cash Crops of India

Choose the correct cash crop in each of the statements below.

1 Sugarcane/Beetroot has a sweet juice which makes a refreshing drink. It is grown in Uttar Pradesh, Karnataka, Tamil Nadu and other states of India.

Beetroot

Sugarcane

Coir

Cotton

2 Coir/Cotton is used to make clothing, home linen, etc. It is grown in Maharashtra, Gujarat, Madhya Pradesh, Karnataka and other states of India.

3 Tea/Lemon is a beverage crop introduced by the British. It is widely grown in Assam and Darjeeling, which are also varieties of this crop.

Tea

Lemon

Cacao

Coffee

4 Cacao/Coffee is a plantation crop that produces a popular beverage. It is grown in Karnataka, Kerala and Tamil Nadu.

5 Soybean/Mustard is a small oilseed grown in Rajasthan, Haryana, Madhya Pradesh and Uttar Pradesh. It is also used as a spice when cooking.

Soyabean

Mustard

Coconut

Castor seed

6 Coconut/Castor seed is an oilseed from trees that grow in the southern coastal regions of India. The fruit makes a refreshing drink when it is not yet ripe.

7 Jute/Linen is used to make gunny bags, ropes, mats, etc. and is grown in West Bengal, Bihar, Assam, Odisha and Meghalaya.

Jute

Linen

Sunflower

Daffodil

8 Sunflower/Daffodil is an oilseed grown in Karnataka, Maharashtra and Andhra Pradesh. The plant has bright yellow blooms.

Whiz quiz

Choose the right options about black pepper, one of the most traded cash crops since antiquity.

1. The scientific name for black pepper is *piper nigrum*/*album*. It contains the chemical compound *capstaicin*/*piperine*, which gives it its hotness quotient.
2. Black pepper is native to the south-western state of Kerala/Tamil Nadu.
3. It is the most traded spice in the world and is served on dining tables everywhere along with salt/sugar.
4. Mexico/Vietnam is the world's biggest exporter of black pepper today.

Whiz fact

India is the largest producer of oilseeds in the world. About 20% of the world's oilseed-producing area is in India.

Literacy Skills

24 Inventors as Nouns

Many of the words we use today are actually the names of inventors, whose inventions became so popular that the words entered the English language as nouns.

Use the clues given below to locate the names of these inventions in the word grid.

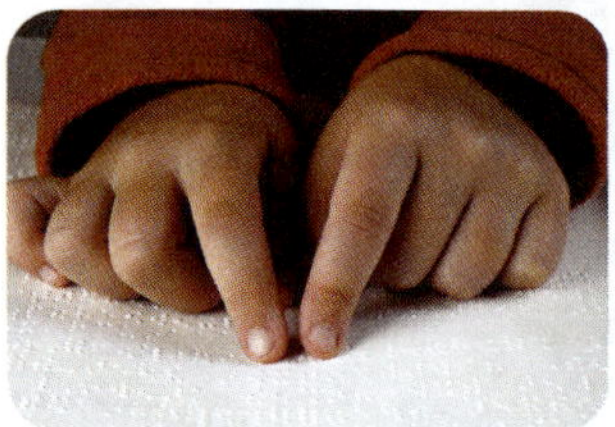

1. Louis .... was a French educator who gave his name to a form of written language for the blind where dots made on thick paper create a code.

2. This system of exercises using a special apparatus got its name from Joseph ...., a German-born physical fitness specialist.

3. Russian lieutenant and small arms designer Mikhail .... created the sub-machine gun AK-47 for the Soviet Army.

4. William .... was a hatter who created this hat to protect the heads of gamekeepers from low-hanging branches while on horseback.

5. Frenchman Jules .... was a trapeze artist whose signature performance costume is worn today by ballerinas and gymnasts worldwide.

6. When a family member suffered severe arthritis, seven innovative .... brothers, Italian immigrants to the US, invented a hydrotherapy pump for the bath to help ease the pain.

7 Rudolf .... was a German mechanical engineer famous for his invention of the internal-combustion engine that bears his name.

8 Robert John Lechmere .... was an Englishman who discovered the guppy fish in 1866.

9 French mathematician and physicist André Marie .... was one of the main discoverers of electromagnetism. He showed that a magnetic field is created when two parallel wires are charged with electricity.

10 George Washington Gale .... Jr. created the Giant Wheel for the 1893 Chicago World's Columbian Exposition.

E	E	K	S	R	E	L	W	O	B
B	R	A	I	L	L	E	L	R	T
D	E	L	Z	S	P	O	E	E	R
E	P	A	Z	T	E	T	O	G	A
Y	M	S	U	R	I	A	P	D	M
P	A	H	C	Z	A	R	R	D	F
P	M	N	A	Z	E	D	D	I	E
U	A	I	J	S	I	R	R	E	F
G	Z	K	S	L	U	M	P	S	W
T	X	O	P	I	L	A	T	E	S
O	E	V	K	L	E	B	E	L	M

Whiz fact

American judge and horticulturist James Harvey Logan successfully crossed the blackberry and the raspberry in California in 1881 to create the Loganberry.

25 The Glorious Middle East

The transcontinental region that covers Western Asia, Turkey and Egypt is called the Middle East from the European perspective.

Fill in the blanks about the Middle East with the words given in the help box.

1 The ...., the tallest man-made structure in the world, is named after a living person—the President of the United Arab Emirates, Khalifa bin Zayed bin Zultan Al Nahyan.

2 Two thousand years ago, the city of Petra in Jordan was a prominent centre of the now lost Nabataean civilisation. What remains now are the caves, temples and tombs made of pink sandstone, which give the city its popular name of ....

3 ...., believed to be the birthplace of Jesus Christ, is a city in the West Bank.

4 Jericho, located in the West Bank, shows evidence that hunters of the Mesolithic period were present as far back as ...., making it one of the earliest continuous settlements in the world.

5 The .... lies between Israel and Jordan. It is almost ten times as salty as the ocean, as a result of which there is no life in it. This is why it has been called so.

6 Babylon was a major city of the Mesopotamian civilisation that flourished along the Euphrates river. For a while, it was the largest city in the world, perhaps the first city to reach a population above ....
One of the seven ancient wonders of the world, the .... was believed to have been located here.

7 The .... connects the Mediterranean Sea to the Red Sea. It was opened in 1869 and helped ships to avoid sailing around Africa using a direct route between Europe and South Asia.

8 ...., a port city in Yemen, was a major coffee exporting centre. Beans transported from other inland regions were shipped abroad from this port. Till today, this coffee is famous worldwide.

9 The .... was a writing tool made of reeds that was first used by the ancient Mesopotamians, to make wedge-shaped marks on ...., called cuneiform.

10 The .... in Egypt is the world's largest dam, built to contain the raging waters of the world's longest river, the ....

Help box

Suez Canal | 9000 BCE | Dead Sea | stylus | Mocha | Aswan Dam | Hanging Gardens of Babylon | Nile | Bethlehem | Rose City | clay tablets | 200,000 | Burj Khalifa

Whiz fact

Saudi Arabia is the largest country in the Middle East and it is the largest country with no rivers. Though over 90% of the country is desert, it imports sand and camels from Australia!

STEM

26 The Story of Penicillin

Penicillin was one of the world's first antibiotic and its discovery marked a turning point in history because doctors finally had a tool that could completely cure their patients of deadly infectious diseases.

Here are some facts about the story of penicillin. Fill in the blanks with words from the help box.

1 Penicillin was discovered by .... in 1928 when he found mould growing in his petri dishes of bacteria at the hospital in London where he worked.

2 He examined the petri dishes and noticed that a mould called .... had prevented the normal growth of the *staphylococci* bacteria.

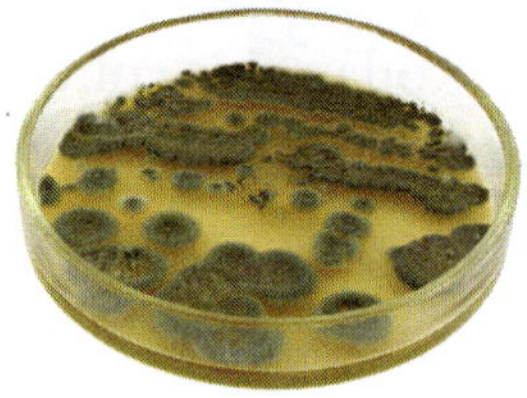

3 He needed to grow more of the mould to be sure that it suppressed the growth of .... Then maybe it could also be used to fight infectious diseases.

4 In 1938, Dr Howard Florey of .... found Dr Fleming's paper on the *Penicillium* moulds and developed a series of penicillium-mould extracts with biochemist Dr Ernst Chain.

5 In 1940, Drs Florey and Chain infected 50 mice with deadly *Streptococcus*. The mice who had received penicillin .... survived while the other half died.

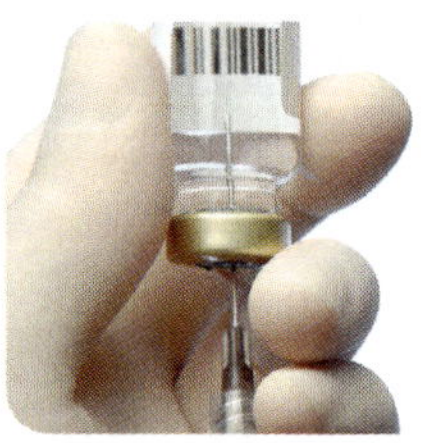

Whiz fact

Dr Heatley was overlooked for the Nobel Prize. In 1990, the University of Oxford made up for this oversight by awarding Heatley the first honorary Doctorate of Medicine awarded to a non-medic in its 800-year history.

6 The cure meant that they needed .... of mould culture fluid to get enough penicillin to treat one person.

7 Biochemist Dr Heatley was trying to develop ways to purify the penicillin so that infections could be treated with lower quantities of a stronger antibiotic. In 1941, Drs Florey and Heatley flew to the United States to develop a means of .... penicillin.

8 Laboratory assistant Mary Hunt found a cantaloupe covered with the fungus *Penicillium chrysogenum*, which yielded .... the amount of penicillin as the species that Dr Fleming had found.

9 *Penicillium chrysogenum* when enhanced with .... and filtration, produced 1,000 times as much penicillin as the first batches from *Penicillium notatum*. The death rate from bacterial infection, which had been 18% in World War I, fell to less than .... in World War II as a result of penicillin.

10 In 1945, Fleming, Florey and Chain were awarded the ....

Help box

1% | University of Oxford | mass producing | *penicillium notatum* | Nobel Prize for Physiology or Medicine | 2,000 litres | X-rays | bacteria | 200 times | injections | Alexander Fleming

Whiz quiz

Answer the following questions.

1 Where is penicillin found? ....

2 Who first discovered that mould could kill bacteria? ....

3 What do antibiotics treat infections from? ....

Literacy Skills

27 Newspapers of India

Earlier, newspapers and magazines were the only way for people to know about what was going on in the world. The first newspaper in India was circulated in 1780 under the editorship of James Augustus Hicky, named *Hicky's Bengal Gazette.*

Use the clues in Column A to find the names of the first newspapers in various Indian regional languages in Column B.

Column A	Column B
1 Published in Chennai (then Madras) from 1882 to 1985 by Indian nationalist G Subramania Iyer	a *Utkala Deepika* in Odia
2 A weekly newspaper published by the Baptist Missionary Society from 1818 to 1841	b *Golconda Patrika* in Telugu
3 Published from 1832 to 1840, this bilingual paper was founded by Balshastri Jambhekar when he was only 20 years old.	c *Mangaluru Samachara* in Kannada
4 This newspaper, published from Hyderabad, was launched in 1926 by Suravaram Pratap Reddy.	d *Swadesamitran* in Tamil
5 This newspaper, published from 1822 to 1888 from Kolkata, was written in a language which actually took shape and developed in Uttar Pradesh.	e *Darpan* in Marathi and English
6 The first state in Northeast India to start publishing a daily local newspaper in 1932	f *Samachar Darpan* in Bengali
7 First printed on 4th August 1866, it is the reason that the 4th of August is celebrated as Odia Journalism Day.	g *Dainik Manipur Patrika* in Manipuri
8 German Rev. Hermann Friedrich Mögling of the Basel Mission started this newspaper in 1843.	h *Jam-i-Jahan-Numa* in Urdu

Whiz fact

In 1826, *Udant Martand*, the first Hindi-language newspaper published in India, started from Calcutta (now Kolkata). It was published every Tuesday.

World Around Us

28 Founders of the Nation

These are some images of the founding fathers of nations around the world. Locate their names in the word grid. To help you, we have given the first letters as well as the number of letters in their names.

L_ _ / K_ _ _ / Y_ _
Singapore

G_ _ _ _ _ _ / K_ _ _
Mongolia

S_ _ / N_ _ _ _ _
Namibia

K	G	P	R	S	I	S	N	G	I	P	R
W	E	Y	N	A	U	K	E	E	L	R	E
A	N	S	W	M	N	A	W	E	T	I	I
M	G	U	H	N	H	N	C	H	M	M	R
E	H	N	A	U	E	D	A	O	U	O	R
N	I	Y	T	J	R	E	N	W	S	Z	E
K	S	K	G	O	E	R	N	E	T	T	F
R	K	T	O	M	T	B	O	V	B	R	N
U	H	S	E	A	H	E	T	E	E	U	A
M	A	E	S	N	A	R	D	R	D	B	H
A	N	N	O	I	T	G	O	I	O	A	O
H	T	C	H	I	L	I	N	H	N	R	J

J_ _ _ _ / F_ _ _ _ _ _
Suriname

S_ _ _ _ _ _ _ _ _ _
Albania

K_ _ _ _ / N_ _ _ _ _ _
Ghana

Whiz fact

Simon Bolivar (1783–1830) led most of South America to freedom in the early 19th century. He is called 'El Libertador' or the 'The Liberator' and can be regarded as the founder of the modern nations of Venezuela, Bolivia, Colombia, Ecuador, Peru and Panama.

Natural World

29 Bird Beaks

All birds have feathers and all birds also have beaks, which they use to feed, defend themselves, groom themselves, feed their young, mate, regulate their body temperature and build nests.

Read the descriptions of the beaks and match them to the birds.

Description

1. When these birds dip their flat beaks in the water to take in food, all the water falls out from the sides.
2. Its thin, needle-like beak helps the bird look for nectar in flowers and suck it in.
3. Their narrowing beak helps them catch prey like insects, small birds and frogs. They also bang their beak to communicate.
4. These birds eat fish, shellfish, octopus, etc. and have a slim, long beak to catch their prey.
5. These birds eat with their head upside down. The curved top part of the beak scoops the food and the tongue presses down to remove extra water.

Birds

a 

Flamingo

b 

Penguin

c 

Hummingbird

d 

Duck

e 

Stork

6 Shaped like a short cone, the thick beak of these birds are great for opening seeds.

7 This bird has the longest beak, which helps it remove extra water when it catches fish. It also keeps predators at bay.

8 The curved beak of this bird has a very sharp tip, which makes it easy for the bird to tear its prey into bite-sized portions.

9 Its thin and long beak helps the bird to pluck insects for food.

10 This bird uses its short and slim beak to pick seeds and eat fruits and plants.

f 

Dove

g 

Sparrow

h 

Pelican

i 

Hawk

j 

Warbler

Whiz fact

Curlew has a beak that is longer than its body. Toucans use their huge beaks to regulate their body temperature.

Curlew

Toucan

India Focus

30 Indian Railways

The Indian Railway Network not only offers transport across cities, but also operates suburban services in several Indian cities and metro services in Kolkata.

Use the clues and help box to solve the crossword about the Indian Railways.

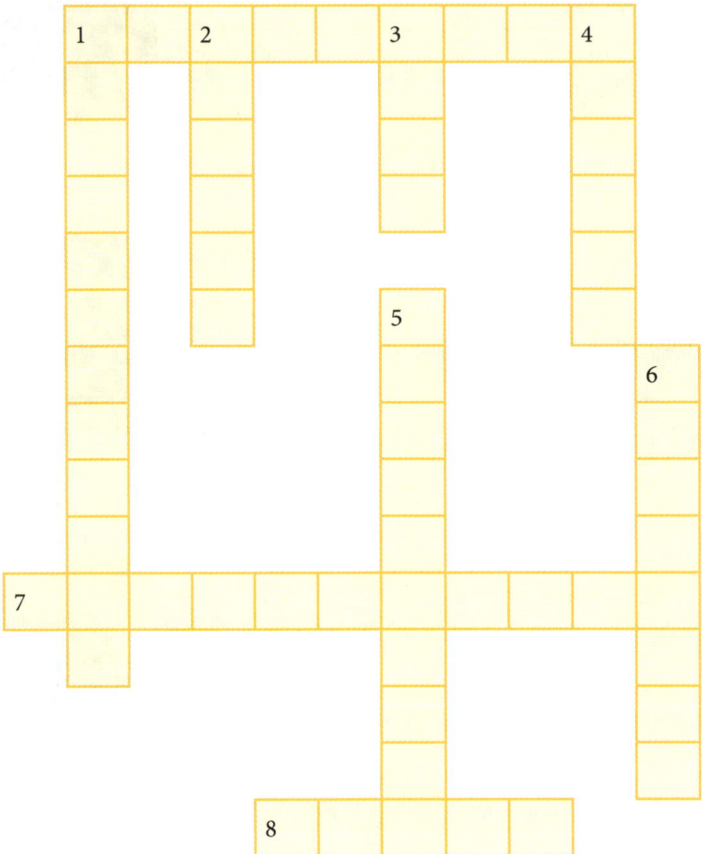

Across

1 The train with the longest route is the Vivek Express which runs between .... and Kanyakumari, covering over 4,200 km.

7 This train runs between Mumbai and Pune.
....

8 Today, the Indian Railways operates across 19 ...., has more than 15 lakh employees and runs 13,000 passenger trains daily.

Down

1 The Sinhagad Express was India's first .... train.

2 The first train journey in India was made on 16 April 1853 from here to Thane.

....

3 The highest railway station in India, it is on the route of the Darjeeling Himalayan Railway. ....

4 The first Rajdhani Express ran between here and Delhi in 1969.

....

5 Manufactured in England in 1855 and used to transport soldiers during the First War of Independence (1857–58), this is the oldest locomotive in the world that is still in use.

....

6 Locomotives are made in .... and Chittaranjan.

Help box

Bombay	Deccan Queen	Dibrugarh	Double Decker
Fairy Queen	Ghum	Howrah	Varanasi
Zones			

Whiz quiz

The 1853 train to Thane was drawn by three engines. They were .... (a term of respect), ... (a province now in Pakistan) and .... (a word for high king or ruler).

Whiz fact

Kavach is an indigenously developed technology that prevents trains from colliding with each other. It does this by installing electronic devices in trains that monitor movement and lapses. It was introduced in March 2022.

Sports

31 Sporting Terms

Terms like goal, point and foul are common across many sports but some terms are specific to certain sports.

Use the help box to fill in the name of the sport associated with each term.

1 Nutmeg is a term used in .... It is a skill to kick the ball through an opposing player's legs before running past them.

2 A pugilist is someone who practises .... The word comes from the Latin word *pugil,* which in turn originates from *pugnus*, meaning fist.

3 When a minor rule is broken in ...., a scrum is a way of restarting play. A scrum is when up to eight players from each team try to get the ball.

4 A cow corner is an area on the .... field where shots were so rarely hit that cows could graze there in peace. In the newest format of the game, the cow corner is a key scoring area.

5 Let is a term in ...., which means a serve has to be replayed because it touched the net.

6 The path on which .... is done is called a *piste*. The term comes from the French word for 'race track'.

7 In ...., an alley-oop is when a player throws a pass to a teammate who catches the ball in mid-air and then dunks it into the basket.

8 In ...., a birdie means a score of one stroke under par. In early 20th century American slang, 'bird' meant anything excellent.

Help box

cricket tennis skiing rugby golf basketball football boxing

Whiz fact

A 'round robin' is one way of conducting a tournament. In this format, each contestant plays all the other contestants. The ICC World Cup 2023 was one such example of round robin tournament.

32 Parliaments of the World

In a democratic form of government, the supreme legislative body is called the Parliament. It is also the executive governing body of the country.

Match the clue with the image and use the help box to write the name of the parliament building of each country below these images.

1. The Indian Parliament House is a curved red sandstone building with 144 columns.
2. The Dutch Parliament is situated next to a pond and was originally a castle. It began to be used as a political centre as far back as 1584.
3. The United Kingdom's Houses of Parliament are situated along the River Thames and have the famous clock Big Ben at one end of the premises.
4. The US Parliament is a white building with many columns and a large, tiered dome.
5. The Parliament of Canada has the tall Peace Tower exactly at the centre. The tower features a clock and has a flagpole on top.
6. New Zealand's Parliament building resembles the home of busy insects.

a 

....

b 

....

c 

....

d 

....

e 

....

f 

....

Help box

Sansad Bhavan | States General | Palace of Westminster | The Centre Block | The United States of Congress | The Beehive

India Focus

33 Northeast India Stars

Northeast India has many personalities who have made great contributions in their fields.

Look at the images and clues and choose the correct name.

1. This six-time Women's World Amateur Boxing champion and Olympic bronze medallist, MC Mary Kom/Laishram Sarita Devi was portrayed by Priyanka Chopra on the screen.

2. The first chief minister of Assam and a Bharat Ratna recipient, the Guwahati international airport is named after Tarun Gogoi/Gopinath Bordoloi.

3. Born Tshering Phintso, he changed his name to Danny Denzongpa/Diganta Hazarika and played the role of Kancha China, the villain in Mukul Anand's *Agneepath*.

4. Aruna Reddy/Dipa Karmakar was the first Indian gymnast to qualify for the Olympics and is one of only five athletes in the world to have successfully performed the incredibly difficult Produnova vault.

5. Rani Gaidinliu/Kanaklata Baruah was jailed at the age of 16 by the British for her role in the freedom struggle. She was given the title of Queen by Jawaharlal Nehru.

6. Bhupen Hazarika/Zubeen Garg was a legendary singer, composer, lyricist and film director who was awarded the Padma Vibhushan, Dadasaheb Phalke Award and National Award for best music director, as well as the Bharat Ratna in 2019.

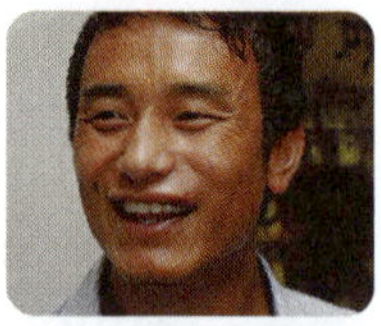

7. The first Indian footballer to sign a contract with a European club, Baichung Bhutia/Aiborlang Khongjee has a stadium named after him in Sikkim.

8. Sheela Borthakur/Indira Goswami was a prominent poet and writer from Assam who was awarded the Sahitya Akademi Award and the Jnanpith Award, among many others.

Whiz fact

Bir Tikendrajit Singh of Manipur was a patriot and prince of the kingdom, who fought the British and precipitated the Anglo-Manipur War of 1891.

Sports

34 Kick-off Time!

Many countries have their own domestic football playing league. Choose the country to which each league belongs.

1 Liga MX (1943) is the domestic football league of Spain/Mexico.

2 India/Italy has the I League (2007).

3 Super Lig (1959) is the name of Portugal's/Turkey's domestic league.

4 Germany's/Argentina's domestic league is called Bundesliga (1962).

5 Serie A (1898) is the domestic football league of Mexico/Italy.

6 Primera Division (1891) is the domestic football league of Argentina/Mexico.

7 Premier Soccer League (1996) is the name of the domestic league of South Africa/USA.

8 France's/Belgium's domestic league is called Ligue 1 (1932).

9 A-League (2004) is the domestic football league of Australia/Argentina.

10 J1 League (1993) is the name of Japan's/The Netherlands' domestic league.

11 Eredivisie (1956) is the domestic league of the Netherlands/Germany.

12 La Liga (1929) is the domestic football league of Spain/Argentina.

Whiz quiz

The most recent Euro Cup (officially the UEFA EURO 2024) was held across nine cities in .... A total of 24 .... participated, with a few notable absentees, including ...., which was banned from participation because of its invasion of Ukraine. A total of 51 .... were played, and 117 .... were scored. .... won the Cup, after defeating England 2-1 in the final match.

STEM

35 Sci-fi Predictions

Science fiction fascinates us because it shows us the possibilities of technological progress. When we look back, many things we take for granted today existed only in the imagination of writers of an earlier time.

Choose the correct option.

1. The 1970s TV show *Star Trek: The Next Generation* introduced a fictional touch-screen computer that was used to share information. This technology became reality with the iPad/Personal Digital Assistant (PDA).

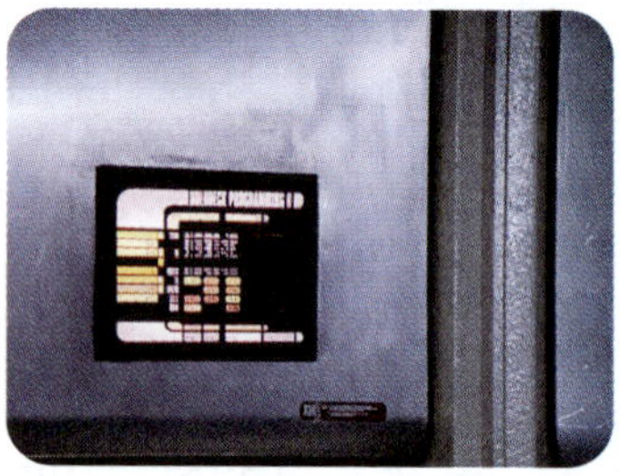

2. In 1870, Jules Verne wrote *Journey to the Centre of the Earth*/*Twenty Thousand Leagues Under the Sea*, in which Captain Nemo travels the oceans in a giant electric submarine called Nautilus. This was the predecessor of submarines like Alvin, made in 1964.

3. William Gibson published *Neuromancer* in 1984 and brought the word artificial intelligence/cyberspace into focus. In the book, this term was a 'consensual hallucination' created by millions of interlinked computers.

4. In 1962, Arthur C Clarke worked with Stanley Kubrick on the film *Full Metal Jacket*/*2001: A Space Odyssey*, which predicted things such as reading newspapers on a digital tablet.

Whiz quiz

Each of these realities has been predicted in these books. Match them.

1	Bionic limb	a	*The Hitchhiker's Guide to the Galaxy*
2	Credit cards	b	*Cyborg*
3	Modern transplants	c	*Looking Backward*
4	Audio translating apps	d	*Frankenstein*

5 In 1911, Hugo Gernsback wrote about machine translation and bone conduction/radio wave hearing devices. In the late 1970s, bone-anchored hearing aids were released using osseointegration technology.

6 The 1982 film *Blade Runner* introduced FaceTime/video conferencing, which allows users in different locations to have face-to-face meetings with each other. The technology was not so widespread then.

7 In 1899, H G Wells' *The Sleeper Awakes* has something resembling a video library with a 'peculiar cylinder' that is put into a USB-type/VCR-type machine.

8 Isaac Asimov wrote several stories about robots and even compiled the Laws of Robotics, long before a robot was ever created. Honda named its robot ASIMO/ISAAC after him.

9 In his book *From the Earth to the Moon*, Jules Verne predicted that man would travel to Mars/Moon. In fact, many parts of the novel were eerily similar to the real first landing.

Whiz fact

Jules Verne successfully predicted lunar modules, capsules attached to rockets that carry people to space. He called them 'projectiles' in his book *From the Earth to the Moon*.

Learning Skills

36 Countries Working Together

Many countries form organisations to work together towards common goals.

COLLABORATION

Given below are statements about some international organisations. Fill in the blanks with words/phrases from the help box, which has some extra words.

1 The North Atlantic Treaty Organisation (NATO) is a security alliance of 30 countries from .... whose fundamental goal is to safeguard the Allies' freedom and security by political and military means.

2 The Association of Southeast Asian Nations (ASEAN) is a regional grouping that promotes economic, political and security cooperation among its .... members.

3 BRICS is the acronym that refers to the five countries, namely Brazil, Russia, India, China and South Africa, which are deemed to be at a similar stage of newly advanced ....

BRICS

4 The South Asian Association for Regional Cooperation (SAARC) was formed to promote .... of the people of South Asian countries.

5 The Caribbean Community (CARICOM) is an organisation of .... Caribbean nations and dependencies whose main objective is to promote economic integration and cooperation among its members and coordinate foreign policy.

6 The Organisation of Petroleum Exporting Countries (OPEC) is an intergovernmental organisation of 13 members that influences prices in the .... and therefore, the economic growth and development of member countries.

7 BIMSTEC, the Bay of Bengal Initiative for Multi-Sectoral Technical and Economic Cooperation, comprises seven nations of .... to promote and encourage specific cooperation projects in trade, agriculture, energy, technology, etc.

Help box

North America	Europe and Africa	economic development	political development		
Middle East	10	education	North America and Europe	2	world oil market
welfare	15	Bangladesh, India, Myanmar, Sri Lanka, Thailand, Nepal and Bhutan			

Whiz fact

The Non-Aligned Movement (NAM) is a forum of 120 developing countries that are not formally aligned with or against any major power bloc. After the United Nations, it is the largest grouping of countries worldwide.

India Focus

37 Tiger Conservation in India

Project Tiger was initiated in 1973. It has been undertaken by approximately 50 national parks and as a result, the tiger population in the wild has seen considerable increase.

Draw lines and match the names of the tiger reserves with their description.

a It derives its name from the abundance of Semul or red silk cotton trees that bloom abundantly in this region in Odisha.

b This national park in Karnataka is also famous for its sandalwood trees.

c A river of the same name flows through the heart of this national park in Assam.

d The barasingha is known as the 'jewel' of this reserve in Madhya Pradesh.

e This reserve in Uttar Pradesh shares a boundary with Nepal.

f This reserve is named after a fort that was built in the 10th century in Rajasthan.

g Rudyard Kipling's *The Jungle Book* was based on this sanctuary spread across parts of Maharashtra and Madhya Pradesh.

h This reserve in Uttarakhand is named after a hunter-turned-conservationist who was a colonel in the British Army.

Whiz fact

The tiger is the biggest member of the cat family. They are the only cat species that are completely striped. They even have stripes on their skin.

Natural World

38 Man-made Disasters

Powerful technology benefits us a lot, but it also has the power to cause great harm. As a result, man-made disasters are only increasing in the scale of harm they cause.

Use the words from the help box to fill in the blanks. Be careful, there are more words than blanks!

1 The .... of 1984 was the worst industrial accident at the time, not just in India, but the world. It was caused by a chemical leak at an insecticide plant owned by the Union Carbide Corporation. Over 15,000 people died, while survivors developed respiratory problems and blindness.

2 The largest .... in history occurred in 2010. There was an explosion on an oil rig in the Gulf of Mexico off the coast of Louisiana. It contaminated the ocean waters, killing thousands of marine animals.

3 The Chernobyl disaster of 1986 is one of the worst man-made disasters in history. One of the .... of the Chernobyl Nuclear Power Plant in Ukraine exploded. The radiation from this affected life for hundreds of kilometres around it, with many people developing deformities and suffering from various types cancers.

4 2018 was the year of the California fires. The Hill Fire and the Woolsey Fires originated in the Thousand Oaks region of California. Over .... people had to leave their homes to prevent being burnt alive and millions suffered from various types of respiratory problems.

Help box

nuclear reactors | machinery | 250,000 | Bhopal Disaster | 10,000 | marine oil spill | fire

Whiz fact

Australia is prone to bushfires, which have gotten more widespread and more frequent thanks to human intervention. Since 2020, over 3 billion animals perished in these deadly fires.

India
Focus

39 Indian Vocalists

Indian vocalists from Hindustani and Carnatic music traditions have delighted audiences across the world since time immemorial.

Identify them from their pictures and descriptions and fill in the blanks, in each case with the same letter.

1 This Carnatic music vocalist is the only singer who has been accorded the title Asthana Gayakan (official singer) of the state of Kerala.

K J YE........UDA........

2 This Hindustani classical vocalist was one of the first female singers to give public concerts. She is still revered as the Mallika-e-Ghazal (Queen of Ghazals).

BEGUM ....KHT........R

3 A legendary Carnatic singer, she was called 'Queen of Music' by Pt. Jawaharlal Nehru and was the first Indian to receive the Ramon Magsaysay Award, often considered Asia's Nobel Prize.

M S ....UBBULAK........HMI

4 Hindustani classical vocalist Shivaputra Siddaramayya Komkalinath was given the title of 'musical spirit' in Hindu mythology because of his great talent. He adopted this as the name by which he is known.

KUM........R G........NDH........RV........

5 He was a Carnatic singer and the only South Indian artist who was invited to sing Tagore's Rabindra Sangeet on All India Radio to preserve it for posterity.

M B........ L .... MUR....... LIKRISHN........

6 This colossus of Hindustani classical music also had a passion for swimming, yoga and football.

BHIM........EN JO........HI

7 This stalwart classical Carnatic vocalist's name was shortened to MLV, said to stand for melody, *laya* and *vidwat*, translated as melody, rhythmic variation and depth of feeling—the essential components of music.

M L V........S........NTH........ KUM........RI

8 This Hindustani classical vocalist is known for her *khayals*, *thumris* and bhajans and was awarded the Padma Shri at the age of 25.

P........RVEEN SULT........N........

Whiz quiz

Four vocalists have been awarded the Bharat Ratna. If two of them were MS Subbulakshmi and Bhimsen Joshi, who were the other two?

1 L...................... M...

2 B..................................... H...

Whiz fact

MS Subbulakshmi, DK Pattammal and ML Vasanthakumari were popularly referred to as the 'female trinity of Carnatic music'.

40 Women Nobel Laureates in Science

In the 120 years since the first Nobel Prize was first awarded, women have won very few prizes in science. But in this millennium, the number of women scientists making important breakthroughs has increased, inspiring more girls to take up research in STEM streams.

Using the statements about Nobel Prize-winning women scientists, identify the discipline for which the Prize was awarded, by choosing between the options in each.

1. Frances Arnold received the Nobel Prize in Physics/Chemistry in 2018 for the directed evolution of enzymes and shared it with George P Smith and Gregory Winter.

2. Barbara McClintock was awarded a solo Nobel Prize in Physics/Medicine in 1983 for her discovery of mobile genetic elements.

3. Ada E Yonath was awarded the Nobel Prize in Physics/Chemistry in 2009, which she shared with Venkatraman Ramakrishnan and Thomas A Steitz for studies on the structure and function of the ribosome.

4. Dorothy Crowfoot Hodgkin was awarded the Nobel Prize in Physics/Chemistry in 1964 for her determinations by X-ray techniques of the structures of important biochemical substances. Five years later, she determined the structure of insulin, a huge medical breakthrough.

5. Donna Strickland was awarded the Nobel Prize in Physics/Medicine in 2018, which she shared with Gérard Mourou of France for their method of generating high-intensity, ultra-short optical pulses and American Arthur Ashkin for the optical tweezers and their application to biological systems.

6 Gertrude B Elion shared the Nobel Prize in Chemistry/ Medicine in 1988 with James W Black and George H. Hitchings for their discoveries of important principles for drug treatment.

7 Tu Youyou shared the Nobel Prize for Chemistry/ Medicine in 2015 with William C Campbell of USA and Satoshi Omura of Japan for her discoveries concerning a novel therapy against malaria.

8 Rita Levi Montalcini from Italy and USA shared the Nobel Prize in Chemistry/Medicine in 1986 with Stanley Cohen (USA) for their discoveries of growth factors.

9 Elizabeth Blackburn from Australia/USA and Carol W Greider from USA shared the Nobel Prize in Physics/ Medicine in 2009 with Jack W Szostak (USA) for discovering how chromosomes are protected by telomeres and the enzyme telomerase.

10 Linda B Buck is an American who shared the Nobel Prize in Physics/Medicine in 2004 with Richard Axel for their discoveries of odorant receptors and the organisation of the olfactory system.

Whiz fact

Women scientists are increasingly being recognised by the scientific community after centuries of being in the shadows. The 2023 Nobel Prize in Physics was shared by Anne L'Huillier for her work on experimental methods that generate attosecond (one-quintillionth) pulses of light for the study of electron dynamics in matter. The Physiology Prize was shared by Katalin Karikò with Drew Weissman for discoveries leading to the development of vaccines against COVID-19.

World Around Us

41 Socotra

The Socotra archipelago consists of four islands, the largest of which is Socotra. Though politically a part of Yemen, the archipelago is geographically a part of Africa.

Use the images and the help box to fill in the blanks.

1. Socotra's mushroom-shaped .... is an unofficial symbol of the island. Its red sap was used as dye in ancient times. Today, it is used in painting, making breath freshener and lipstick and also for varnishing violins.
2. .... are the only mammals endemic to Socotra.
3. The sea snail .... is found here. The shells of these creatures were valuable and used as jewellery and currency in the past.
4. The aptly named .... is endemic to Socotra, with its thick base filled with fluid and narrow neck at the top. Its thick fleshy leaves also allow it to hold liquid.
5. Socotra has many types of reptiles, including .... , which are lizards that look more like snakes, but with very small limbs.
6. The Socotran .... is one of the island's endemic species. Its cousins can be found throughout most of the world, but this variety can be found only here.
7. Socotra's name is traced to the Sanskrit *dvipa-sakhadara*, or the ....

Help box

Bats | bottle tree | cowry | Dragon's Blood tree | island of bliss | skinks | starling

Whiz fact

Socotra is considered one of the most alien-looking places on Earth. It is the most biodiverse place in the Arabian Sea and is a UNESCO World Heritage Site because one-third of its endemic flora and fauna are found nowhere else on Earth.

India Focus

42 Indian Directors

India produces most films in a year—as many as 1600 in various languages.

Read the description and write the name of the state from which the languages in which these famous directors made the films originated. Then draw lines and match the states on the map.

1. Adoor Gopalakrishnan revolutionised Malayalam cinema and has been awarded the Dadasaheb Phalke Award, the Padma Shri and the Padma Vibhushan.
....

2. Bommireddy Narasimha Reddy made *Malliswari*, the first Telugu film to be screened at international film festivals. ....

3. Bhalji Pendharkar began his career in the 1920s in Bombay and made over 70 films.
....

4. Ritwik Ghatak was born in Dhaka and died in Kolkata. He received the Padma Shri for his contribution to cinema.
....

5. D Rajendra Babu was a filmmaker and screenplay writer known primarily for his Kannada movies.
....

6. Mani Ratnam, born in Chennai, predominantly makes films in Tamil Language. *Mouna Ragam* was the film that made him famous.......................................

Whiz fact

Satyajit Ray is the only Indian filmmaker to have received an Honorary Academy Award (Oscar) for his contribution to cinema. He made films in Bengali and Hindi. *Pather Panchali* (1955) was his first feature film, while *Agantuk* (1992) was his last.

43 Arctic Region

The area around the North Pole is called the Arctic region.

Use the clues and the help box to circle the answers in the grid and fill in the blanks.

W	T	M	P	O	L	A	R
A	I	P	E	R	T	Y	U
L	I	N	U	I	T	S	S
R	S	L	O	C	S	M	S
U	P	A	V	E	N	A	I
S	P	P	A	L	E	N	A
E	D	F	S	A	H	G	Q
R	A	O	P	N	C	K	E
E	R	W	A	D	I	M	X
X	T	L	R	K	L	L	Z

1 The ...., a group of people who live in Norway, Finland and Sweden, are amongst the few who can live in the inhospitable climate of the Arctic.

2 Indigenous people who live in Northern Canada, Alaska (USA) and Greenland (Denmark) are known as ....

3 Of the eight countries in the Arctic Council, two are .... and ....

4 Trees do not grow in the Arctic, but there are thick layers of .... and mosses in several parts of this region.

5 This type of bear is found in the Arctic region.
....

6 This marine mammal is found in the Arctic.
....

Help box

Inuit | Lapps | lichens | Iceland | Russia | Walrus | Polar

Whiz fact

The narwhal is a species found only in the Arctic. It is often called the 'unicorn of the sea' because male narwhals have a straight tusk projecting from the front of their head which can grow to over 3 m in length.

Literacy Skills

44 How Banks Work

FINANCIAL LITERACY

Choose the correct option and complete these statements related to banks.

1 A bank is a place where we get a bond/document/loan to buy a vehicle or for business purposes.

2 A person who uses the services of a bank is said to have an account/allowance/ATM there.

3 You can safely store your valuables like jewellery in a bank box/safe/locker.

4 A person or entity who writes a cheque as payment to another is called a payee/recipient/bearer.

5 The person in whose name a cheque is made out is called the bearer/drawee/holder.

6 A cheque that can be shown so as to get actual cash in currency notes (called encashment) is called a bearer/normal/money cheque.

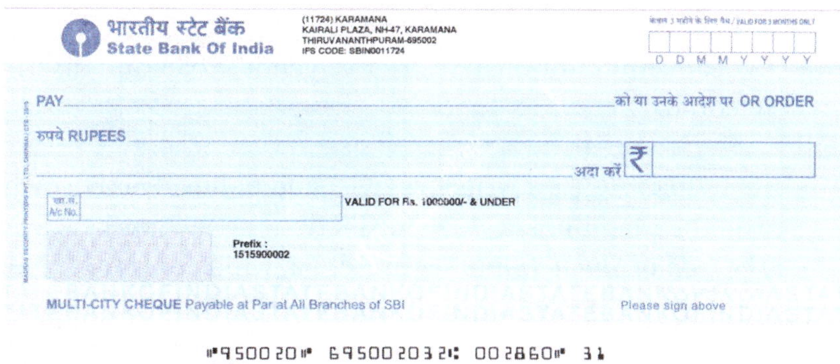

7 A bank normally returns you more money than you deposit because it pays you an extra/indemnity/interest on your deposited money.

8 A recurring/fixed/share deposit allows you to deposit a certain amount of money which the bank returns to you after a certain specified period of time.

9 A cheque must be crossed/signed/empty to show that the amount cannot be paid in cash but must be credited into an account.

10 A cheque can be used to withdraw cash for a period of 3 days/3 weeks/3 months from the date on it.

11 The QR code/cheque number/reference number is a way to uniquely identify each cheque. It is printed in magnetic ink so it can be read by a machine also.

12 Money borrowed from a bank is often returned in the form of monthly payments called EMIs/ATMs/PINs.

Whiz fact

The first bank of India was the Bank of Hindustan, which was established in 1770 and closed down (the technical term is 'liquidated') in 1829–32.

45 Indian Sub-continent Authors

Given below are some famous authors of the Indian sub-continent and the books they are famous for.

Use the help box and write the names of the country these authors are from.

1 Taslima Nasrin is an author and former physician who has been living in Sweden since her exile from her homeland in 1994. She is the author of *Lajja*, meaning 'shame', which tells the story of four women who are victims of male chauvinism, but decided to fight for their rights. ....

2 Kunzang Choden is a writer whose book *The Circle of Karma* is set in the initial period of imperially regulated modernisation in her country, where women have to deal with traditional, restrictive gender roles and discrimination as men gain economic freedom. ....

3 Arundhati Roy is a writer, essayist and political activist who won the Man Booker Prize for Fiction in 1997 for her novel *The God of Small Things* set in Kerala, which tells the childhood experiences of fraternal twins whose lives are destroyed by society that lays down laws about who should be loved, how and how much. ....

4 Ru Freeman is a writer, journalist and activist whose novel *On Sal Mal Lane* talks about the years leading up to the civil war between the Tamils and the Sinhalese. ....

5 Mohsin Hamid is a novelist whose book *Moth Smoke* tells the story of a banker in Lahore who loses his job, falls in love with his best friend's wife and plunges into a life of drugs and crime.

....

6 Author Bishnu Kumari Waiba moved to Kathmandu after her education in India. She is known by her pen name Parijat. Her most famous work is *Shirish ko Phool (The Blue Mimosa)*. This story of an alcoholic ex-soldier depicts the way women are perceived by men and how they are expected to behave in society. ....

Help box

Nepal | Sri Lanka | Bangladesh | Bhutan | India | Pakistan

46 Importing Words

CRITICAL THINKING

Globalisation has made us familiar with many things from different countries and cultures that we would not otherwise know about. As a result, many words have been imported into the English language.

Use the clues and images to find the English word that has evolved from its foreign origins.

Foreign word and meaning	Image	English word
1 *Ustensile* is French for 'cooking tools'.	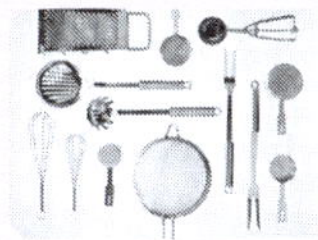	U................................
2 *Ke-stiap* is a Chinese concoction of pickled fish and spices.		K................................
3 *Laimun* is the Arabic word for this yellow citrus fruit.		L................................
4 The Dutch word *koekie* means 'akin to cake'.		C................................
5 The Italian term *cartone* refers to a drawing on hard paper.		C................................
6 The German word *hamastro* refers to a short-tailed, stout-bodied burrowing rodent.		H................................
7 The Hindi *champi* means 'to knead, squeeze or massage'.		S................................
8 The Greek *anõnumos* refers to something or someone without a name.		A................................

Whiz fact

Bon voyage is French for 'have a nice trip'. It is used commonly today to express good wishes to someone about to set off on a journey.

World Around Us

47 The Nobel Peace Prize

As per the will of Swedish inventor and businessman Alfred Nobel, the Peace Prize is awarded "to the person who shall have done the most or the best work for fraternity between nations, for the abolition or reduction of standing armies and for the holding and promotion of peace congresses". The Nobel Peace Prize is the only Nobel Prize that can be awarded to an organisation as well as to individuals.

Here are some important Nobel Peace Prize laureates. Match the years, the descriptive statements and the names of the winners.

Year(s)	Description/Clue	Organisation
1 1917, 1944 and 1963	i This political entity won the prize, because for over six decades (since its formation in 1958), it "contributed to the advancement of peace and reconciliation, democracy and human rights in Europe".	a Grameen Bank 
2 1954 and 1981	ii This organisation has won the Peace Prize the most number of time for its humanitarian work during wartime as well as during the Cold War.	b Médecins Sans Frontières 
3 1999	iii This organisation won the Prize twice for "its efforts to heal the wounds of war by providing help and protection to refugees all over the world" and "for promoting the fundamental rights of refugees".	c European Union 
4 2006	iv This Swiss organisation whose name means 'Doctors without Borders' was awarded the Prize for its humanitarian work across continents, just before the end of the century.	d International Committee of the Red Cross 

5 2012	v This winner from Bangladesh, whose name includes a word that means 'rural' shared the prize with its founder Muhammad Yunus "for their efforts to create economic and social development from below", the same year that Turkey's Orhan Pamuk won the Literature Prize.	e Office of the United Nations High Commissioner for Refugees 
6 2013 and 2017	vi This UN body won the Peace Prize in a world wracked by COVID-19, for its longstanding efforts to end hunger, which can be and has been used as a weapon of war and conflict.	f Intergovernmental Panel on Climate Change 
7 2020	vii US Vice-President Al Gore shared the Nobel Peace Prize with this organisation for their efforts "to build up and disseminate greater knowledge about man-made climate change, and to lay the foundations for the measures that are needed to counteract such change".	g Organisation for the Prohibition of Chemical Weapons & International Campaign to Abolish Nuclear Weapons 
8 2007	viii Two European entities won the Peace Prize four years apart for their efforts in preventing and eliminating the use of chemical and nuclear weapons in a bid to save humanity from catastrophic consequences.	h World Food Programme 

Whiz fact

The Nobel Peace Prize is the only Nobel Prize awarded in Norway, based on a decision taken by the Norwegian Nobel Committee. All the other Nobel Prizes are awarded in Sweden, the home country of Alfred Nobel.

48 Roads and Highways in India

With approximately 6.4 million kilometres of roads criss-crossing the country, India has the second largest road network in the world after the United States. Construction of roads is the responsibility of the Ministry of Road Transport and Highways.

Locate the numbers that are given in the statements on the word grid and find the correct answers. Then fill in the blanks to learn about the roads and highways that have catapulted India into the twenty-first century.

A	B	T	V	A	Y	O	X	[1]T	H	N	[2]L	M	[3]A	W	T	I
C	O	G	C	J	I	P	[4]R	O	H	T	A	N	G	Y	O	P
D	O	W	E	[5]Y	T	E	K	L	A	E	N	B	R	B	Z	S
Y	J	[6]Q	U	A	D	R	I	L	A	T	E	R	A	[7]L	X	[8]K
G	[9]L	B	C	M	U	W	C	F	B	Q	S	B	J	E	B	A
[10]J	A	M	M	U	X	V	B	S	V	B	F	N	G	H	M	R
B	D	E	B	N	Q	S	[11]P	V	C	V	D	A	[12]D	D	C	G
C	A	H	F	A	L	[13]C	O	R	R	I	D	O	R	D	E	I
O	K	K	D	J	B	Y	R	O	X	P	O	W	[14]A	T	A	L
T	H	B	C	N	H	U	B	K	N	Y	[15]S	H	S	K	G	B
[16]M	B	O	P	L	K	[17]M	A	N	A	L	I	B	L	[18]T	A	J
U	H	I	J	[19]S	L	Z	N	J	G	R	L	V	M	W	D	F
M	R	E	F	Y	J	T	D	H	J	Y	C	I	[20]S	E	T	U
[21]B	H	A	R	A	T	M	A	L	A	H	H	V	L	L	P	K
A	G	F	J	M	N	H	R	H	M	H	A	K	M	V	M	N
I	H	I	U	A	M	H	I	L	[22]M	I	R	A	G	E	U	I

1 A road that we pay to use is called a .... (1) road. Every road or highway has space for one to sixteen vehicles running side by side. Each such space is called a .... (2).

2 .... (18) Expressway, originally named after India's most famous tomb, was renamed .... (5) Expressway, after the river that runs through the region. It connects Delhi to .... (3), the capital of Akbar. French military aircraft Dassault .... (22) 2000 landed on this expressway for the first time on 21 May 2015.

3 The .... (7), ... (17) highway is the second highest in the world, connecting the capital of Ladakh and a hill station in Himachal Pradesh.

4 The Golden .... (6), a rough four-sided figure, connects the four megalopolises of India, namely Delhi, Kolkata, Mumbai and Chennai, covering a total distance of 5846 kilometres.

5 .... (21) Pariyojana literally means the "India Garland" Project. With a planned coverage of 83677 kilometres, it is India's umbrella project for the construction of roads everywhere.

6 A section of national highway(s) connecting two major towns or cities is called a .... (13).

7 The north-south corridor is India's longest, running from Srinagar to Kanyakumari, whilst the east-west corridor connects .... (15) in Assam to .... (11), the birthplace of Mahatma Gandhi, in Gujarat.

8 .... (20) Bharatam, literally "India Bridge" is a project that aims to make sure that national highways are free of railway crossings.

9 An expressway is a national highway with limited access. The Delhi-........... (16) expressway, scheduled to be ready by March 2023, will cut travel time between the India's capital city and its financial hub to just .... (18) hours.

10 .... (14) Tunnel, named after a former prime minister of India, was built under the .... (4) Pass in the Pir Panjal Range and inaugurated on 3 October 2020 by Prime Minister Narendra Modi. At 9.02 kilometres, it is the longest highway single-tube tunnel above 10,000 feet in the world.

11 Dr. ....(19) Prasad Mookerjee Tunnel between .... (10) and Srinagar is India's longest road tunnel, reducing the distance between cities by 30 kilometres and time by 2 hours.

12 The Zoji-La Tunnel, currently under construction under the Zoji-La Pass, will connect .... (8), the city that saw a war in 1999, to .... (12), the coldest city in India.

Language and Literature

49 Presenting Prefixes

Long words that are difficult to understand may have prefixes, or part-words that are 'fixed' before a word. Knowing them makes it easier for us to understand their meanings.

Given below are four prefixes and their meanings.

1. Omni – all, of all things, in all places
2. Tele – far, distant
3. Super/Sur – over, above, beyond, greater in quality
4. Pre – before, in front of, early, beforehand

Add one of the above prefixes to each word to make the new word whose meaning is given.

Adding Prefixes	New Words
1 .... + phone	.... – An instrument by which sound is carried over a distance
2 .... + market	.... – A larger form of grocery store, with a greater variety of goods
3 .... + potent	.... – One who is all powerful
4 .... + script	.... – A letter, figure of symbol printed above the line
5 .... + school	.... – Where children go before they join formal school
6 .... + scope	.... – An object that makes distant objects appear closer and, therefore, larger
7 .... + caution	.... – A measure taken in advance to ward off impending danger

Whiz fact

Part-words that are added to words to coin new, more precise terms, are called affixes. These may be prefixes (before), suffixes (after) or infixes (in the middle).

India Focus

50 Indian Diaspora

People who originate from one country and move to other countries are called the diaspora of the original country.

Match the names and images of members of the Indian diaspora with the achievements for which they are known. Then write the correct letter in the boxes given below the images.

1 

Salman Rushdie

2 

Kalpana Chawla

3 

Mira Nair

a Born in Mumbai, he is one of the world's leading conductors.

b Born in Mumbai, he won the Booker Prize for his novel *Midnight's Children* and was knighted by Queen Elizabeth II in 1999.

c This filmmaker was born in Odisha. She won the Golden Camera award at the Cannes Film Festival for her film *Salaam Bombay*.

d Her novel *The Inheritance of Loss* won the Booker Prize in 2006.

e Born in Haryana, she was the first Indian-American astronaut and the first woman of Indian origin in space.

f Born in West Bengal, he is known for his contributions to welfare economics and economic and social justice.

4 

Zubin Mehta

5 

Amartya Sen

6 

Kiran Desai

Whiz fact

Diaspora comes from the Greek word *diaspeirein*, meaning disperse; literally *dia* 'across' and *speirein* 'scatter', or to 'scatter about'.

15 LIFE ON LAND

Life on Land

51 Environmentally Conscious Tourism

Eco-tourism is tourism intended to support conservation efforts. It focuses on socially responsible travel and environmental sustainability. Carbon footprint is the amount of carbon dioxide released into the atmosphere as a result of the activities of a person, organisation or community. Eco-tourism seeks to reduce carbon footprints of all tourists.

From the options offered below, choose the most environmentally responsible one.

1. When you pack to go on vacation, you carry
   a. lots of luggage because you like having your things with you.
   b. exactly enough clothes for your two-week vacation.
   c. a few tops and bottoms that you can mix-and-match, which are easy to wash and dry.

2. When you leave your hotel room to go sightseeing, you switch off
   a. all the lights and the AC.
   b. all electrical equipment and hang a 'Do Not Disturb' sign so that your sheets and towels are not changed.
   c. all electrical equipment.

3. You see many brochures to a number of tourist spots. You
   a. take a copy of each one that interests you and return it when you've visited the site.
   b. take a few and leave them scattered at various places you visit.
   c. grab as many as you can because you don't want to run short.

4. Every morning, as you leave your hotel room, you
   a. have a quick shower.
   b. have a long 30-minute shower.
   c. soak in the tub followed by a quick shower.

5 You eat

a packaged branded food.

b local food served at various eateries.

c exotic food prepared by using endangered species as ingredients.

6 At tourist spots, you

a scratch your name on trees or buildings because you want to leave proof that you visited the place.

b carry samples of leaves, flowers and fruit from trees and hair and feathers from birds and animals as souvenirs.

c take pictures where permitted to remember your trip.

7 When you shop, you look for

a exotic, unusual items because you want to have one before they are no longer available in the world.

b trinkets made by the locals using local materials available in plenty.

c beautifully wrapped packaged goods to give as gifts.

8 The goal of your vacation is

a to experience a place as it is, in all its natural beauty.

b to collect unusual things as proof that you visited the place.

c to leave proof wherever you go, that you visited the place.

9 If you go on a wildlife safari, you

a carry a stout stick with you, just in case an animal attacks you.

b keep your voice low and wear camouflage clothing to merge in the surroundings.

c wear bright-coloured clothing and speak loudly to protect yourself from any wild animals nearby.

Whiz fact

Singer-actor Justin Timberlake got a company to figure out the carbon footprint of his concerts and paid to have trees and bushes planted in those cities to combat the ill effects.

India Focus

52 UNESCO World Heritage Sites in India

The United Nations Educational, Scientific and Cultural Organisation (UNESCO) designates certain sites as World Heritage Sites due to their natural or cultural significance.

Tick (✓) the correct World Heritage Site in each of these sentences.

1. Humayun's/Akbar's Tomb is a UNESCO World Heritage site in New Delhi.

2. The Vindhyas/Western Ghats have been declared a UNESCO World Heritage Site. This will ensure international support for its conservation.

3. The Mandapa of the Five Pandavas, the Shore Temple and the five rathas are part of a group of monuments at Mahabalipuram/Hampi.

4. Kumbhalgarh, Sawai Madhopur, Jaisalmer and Amber are some of the hill forts of Maharashtra/Rajasthan.

5. The Elephanta Caves/Borra Caves house a collection of rock art linked to the cult of Lord Shiva.

6. Manas National Park/Keoladeo National Park is famous for its migratory birds visiting from as far as Turkey, China and Siberia.

7. The churches and convents of Goa/Puducherry are on the World Heritage list for the grandeur, scale and splendour of Portuguese architecture.

8 The Roadways of India/Mountain Railways of India are on the World Heritage list for being outstanding examples of bold, ingenious engineering solutions to tackle the problem of establishing a link through rugged, mountainous terrain.

9 The Jantar Mantar/Kodaikanal Solar Observatory is a collection of architectural astronomical instruments built by Maharaja Jai Singh.

10 The Victorian Gothic and Art Deco buildings of Kolkata/Mumbai are a recent addition to the UNESCO World Heritage list.

11 The Historic City of Ahmedabad/Bhopal was a walled city founded by Sultan Ahmad Shah and it presents a rich architectural heritage from the Sultanate Period.

12 Agrasen ki Baoli in Delhi/Rani ki Vav in Gujarat is a stepwell famous for its size and sculpture. It is featured on the ₹100 currency note.

Whiz quiz

With 42 sites as of 2024, India has the sixth largest number of UNESCO World Heritage Sites. Which countries have higher numbers than India? Write them here. ....
....

Whiz fact

The Vijaya Vittala Temple in Hampi has 56 musical pillars that produce musical tones when struck with a thumb.

STEM

53 Artificial Satellites in Space

Artificial satellites are responsible for many of the comforts of modern life such as communications and GPS.

Use the clues, pictures and help box to solve the crossword.

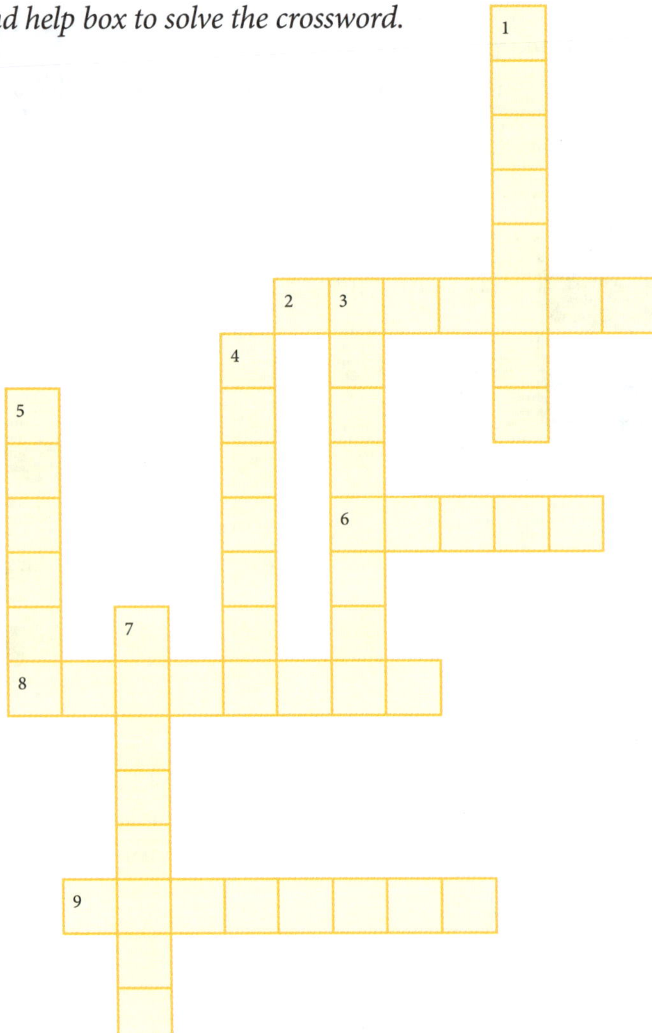

Across

2 AT&T developed the world's first active communications satellite, ... 1. It was launched by NASA in 1962. This satellite allowed the first live broadcast of television images between the United States and Europe.

6 Japan's first artificial satellite was launched in 1970. It was named after the peninsula on which the launch centre is located. It made Japan the fourth country in the world, after the former Soviet Union, the United States and France, to have launched a satellite in to space. ....

8 ....-I was the first experimental remote sensing satellite built in India. It was named after ancient Indian mathematician Bhãskara.

9 This was the first satellite launched from Italy. It was the first of five as part of the Italian-US San Marco programme. ....

Down

1 Canada launched its first research satellite in 1965. This satellite was designed to explore the ionosphere. ....

3 The United States launched its first artificial satellite, ... 1, in 1958.

4 The first artificial satellite was launched for the first time in 1957 by the Soviet Union. It was called .... 1. It was this launch that triggered the Space Race between The Soviet Union and America.

5 This is the first space station launched by NASA. It was launched in 1973 and orbited Earth for six years, allowing scientists to conduct experiments in fields such as biomedical life sciences. ....

7 .... 1 was the fourth artificial Earth orbital satellite to be successfully launched by the United States. This satellite had its own solar electric power and it remains the oldest satellite that is still in orbit.

Help box

Bhaskara | San Marco | Explorer | Alouette | Vanguard | Telstar | Osumi | Sputnik | Skylab

Whiz quiz

India has many extra-terrestrial launches planned in the 2020s. Match these missions with where they plan to go.

1. Aditya-I	a. Moon
2. Shukrayaan	b. Sun
3. Chandrayaan-4	c. Venus

54 Indian Army Insignia

An insignia is a badge of military rank, office or membership of an organisation.

Match the insignia with the Army Officer's Rank and description.

1 

2 

3 

4 

5 

a The Colonel wears the national emblem over 2 five-pointed stars.

b The Lieutenant wears 2 five-pointed stars.

c The Lieutenant Colonel wears the national emblem over a five-pointed star.

d The Field Marshal wears the national emblem over a crossed baton and sabre in a lotus blossom wreath.

e The Major wears the national emblem.

f The Captain wears 3 five-pointed stars.

g The Major General wears a five-pointed star over a crossed baton and sabre.

h The Brigadier wears the national emblem over 3 five-pointed stars in a triangular formation.

i The General wears the national emblem over a five-pointed star, all over a crossed baton and sabre.

j The Lieutenant General wears the national emblem over a crossed baton and sabre.

6 

7 

8 

9 

10 

Whiz fact

The Field Marshal rank is mostly ceremonial. It has been conferred on only two officers in the past: the late Field Marshal Sam Manekshaw and the late Field Marshal K M Cariappa.

Art and Entertainment

55 Famous Indian Artists

Read the description and match the famous Indian artists with their art.

	Artist	Description		Art
1	 S H Raza	The bindu (dot) or shunya (zero) was the focal point of his work and he was known for his huge canvasses.	a	 *Self-portrait*
2	 Amrita Sher-Gil	Her self-portraits are intense and hypnotic, drawing the viewer (that is, us) into the mind of the artist.	b	 *Bindu*
3	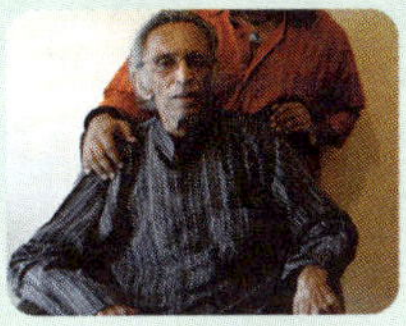 Tyeb Mehta	His work is known for its simple forms and solid colours.	c	 *Shakuntala*
4	 M F Husain	He enjoyed depicting the power and free spirit of horses through bold outlines.	d	 *Mahishasura*
5	 Jamini Roy	He was inspired by the folk art of Bengal and his paintings are known for their vibrant colours and special facial features.	e	 *The Sixth Seal*
6	 Raja Ravi Varma	He is known as the artist who gave Indian gods, goddesses and mythological figures their faces and forms.	f	 *Mother and Child*

World Around Us

56 The "United States of Europe"

European countries fought amongst themselves in the past, but since World War II, they have tried to unite through various initiatives. The European member states are countries that are a part of one or more of the four major treaty groups, namely the European Union (EU), Eurozone, Schengen and NATO.

In this map of Europe, the countries have different colours, which mean different things as shown in the Venn diagram. Read the statements given below and use the map, venn diagram and the help box to fill in the blanks.

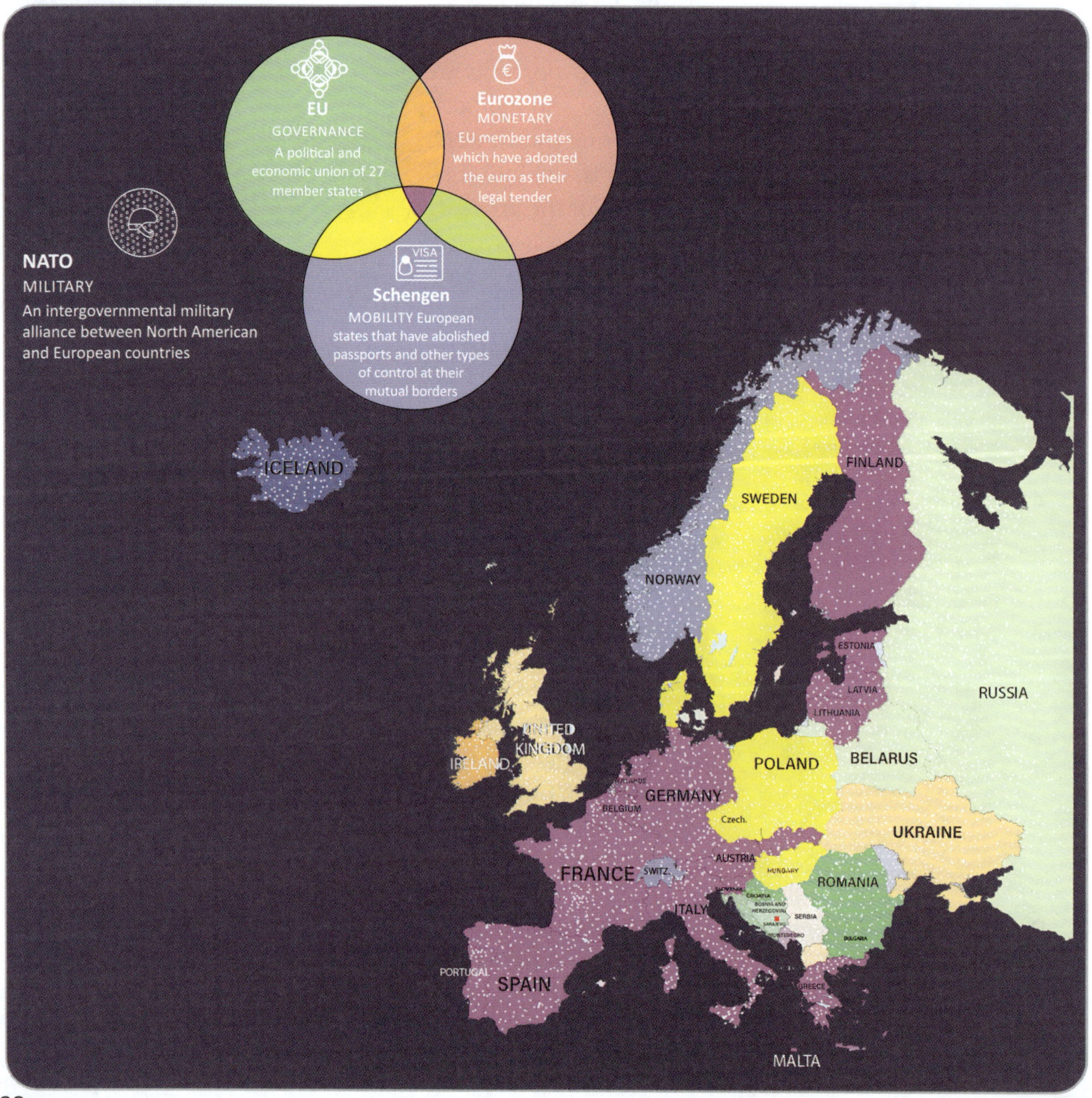

1. A war-torn country as of early 2022, this former Soviet Union nation is now recognised as a candidate for joining the EU. ....
2. This city in Holland hosted an important treaty, following which the European Union was formally established on 1 November 1993. ....
3. This tiny Mediterranean country with strategic naval importance hosted the summit that ended the Cold War. It is part of the EU, Schengen and the Eurozone. ....
4. This country was one of the six founding members of the EEC. Its capital city is also the seat of the European Parliament. ....
5. This language has the maximum number of native speakers in Europe and it is also spoken as a native and/or official tongue in at least six other countries. ....
6. In 2012, the EU won this prize for having "contributed to the advancement of peace and reconciliation, democracy and human rights in Europe." ....
7. Only one Scandinavian country is in the EU, in the Eurozone and also a Schengen country. ....
8. This original EEC member famously exited the EU following a nationwide vote in 2020. ....
9. This country on the Adriatic Sea, situated at the crossroads between Central and Southeast Europe, became the 28th member of the EU in 2013. ....
10. An agreement signed in this town in Luxembourg allows for easy of mobility amongst member countries, as it enables a visa that spans 26 European countries. ....
11. The name of this Scandinavian country implies its northerliness. Although not a member of the EU, it is a member of the Schengen Agreement, as well as the common European Market. ....
12. The only megacity in continental Europe as well as in the EU, this ancient city on the banks of the River Seine has 13 million inhabitants. ....

Help box

Finland, Paris, German, Malta, Nobel Peace Prize, Belgium, Norway, Schengen, United Kingdom, Croatia, Maastricht, Ukraine

Whiz fact

San Marino, is included amongst the Schengen nations primarily because access to it is necessarily through Italy, within which it is an enclave. Similarly, although not an EU or Schengen member, Monaco, the second-smallest country in the world after the Vatican City, uses the Euro as currency.

Quiz Yourself 1

Answer these questions.

1. Which regional grouping promotes economic, political and security cooperation among nations in South East Asia?

   a. BRICS b. ASEAN c. BIMSTEC d. SAARC

2. Which was the first newspaper published in India?

   a. *Hicky's Bengal Gazette* b. *Hindustan*
   c. *Samachar Darpan* d. *Udant Martand*

3. Who is the only Indian gymnast to have successfully performed the incredibly difficult Produnova vault?

   a. Hima Das b. PT Usha
   c. Karnam Malleswari d. Dipa Karmakar

4. What is the nickname given to the narwhal, found only in the Arctic Ocean, on account of its single tusk?

   a. Sea rhino b. Unicorn of the sea
   c. Elephant of the sea d. Sea mammoth

5. What is the name given to the New Zealand parliament, which looks like the home of busy insects?

   a. Anthill b. Nest c. Beehive d. Burrow

6. From which language do we get the word for ketchup?

   a. Chinese b. French c. Arabic d. Swahili

7. Which actor and director revolutionised Malayalam cinema and has been awarded the Dadasaheb Phalke Award, the Padma Shri and the Padma Vibhushan?

   a. Mammootty b. Mohanlal
   c. Priyadarshan d. Adoor Gopalakrishnan

8. What is the Japanese art of flower arrangement called?

   a. Origami b. Ikebana c. Shinto d. Bento

9. The insignia of which military officer features the national emblem over 2 five-pointed stars?

   a. Major b. Lieutenant c. Colonel d. Field Marshal

10. What is the term given to the use of social networks to harm or harass a person?

    a. Cyberbullying b. Phishing c. Pharming d. Stalking

Quiz Yourself 2

Answer these questions.

1 Locomotives are made at two places in India. One is Varanasi. Name the other.

a. Kanyakumari b. Sinhagad c. Chittaranjan d. Howrah

2 When this bird dips its broad and flat beak in the water to take in food, all the water falls out from the sides. Name it.

a. Duck b. Pelican c. Stork d. Flamingo

3 In which national park in Maharashtra is Rudyard Kipling said to have based his story The Jungle Book?

a. Kanha b. Pench c. Tadoba d. Bandhavgarh

4 Which city in Tamil Nadu is called the 'Manchester of South India' because of its extensive textile industry?

a. Kanyakumari b. Madurai c. Trichy d. Coimbatore

5 Which country does Ru Freeman, whose novel *On Sal Mal Lane* talks about the years leading up to the civil war between the Tamils and the Sinhalese, belong to?

a. Singapore b. Sri Lanka c. Maldives d. Malaysia

6 Which Renaissance artist painted the ceiling of the Sistine Chapel in the Vatican City?

a. Leonardo da Vinci b. Raphael

c. Michelangelo d. Vincent van Gogh

7 Which of these cash crops is used to make gunny bags?

a. Jute b. Cotton c. Coir d. Linen

8 Which place cannot join the FIFA because it does not have enough grass?

a. Iceland b. Canada c. Alaska d. Greenland

9 Which book by Jules Verne chronicles the voyages of Captain Nemo?

a. *Journey to the Centre of the Earth* b. *Around the World in Eighty Days*

c. *Twenty Thousand Leagues under the Sea* d. *From the Earth to the Moon*

10 Which portmanteau word is used to shorten "international network?

a. Intel b. Internet c. Interpol d. Intern

Quiz Yourself 3

Answer these questions.

1 Which tree is the unofficial symbol of Socotra?

a. Baobab b. Bottle c. Coconut d. Palm

2 Which UNESCO World Heritage site is a collection of architectural astronomical instruments built by Maharaja Jai Singh?

a. Amber Palace b. Yantra Mandir c. Jantar Mantar d. Yantra Raja

3 In which neighbouring country is the Kutiah glacier?

a. Pakistan b. Nepal c. Bhutan d. Afghanistan

4 Where in Tamil Nadu is the statue of Tamil poet and philosopher Valluvar?

a. Thiruvannamalai b. Sriperumbudur

c. Tirunelveli d. Kanyakumari

5 Which lake makes a boundary between Tanzania and Congo?

a. Victoria b. Tanganyika c. Baikal d. Malawi

6 Which woman scientist shared the Nobel Prize for Medicine in 2015 with two other scientists for her discoveries concerning a novel therapy against malaria?

a. Marie Curie b. Dorothy Hodgkin

c. Rita Levi-Montalcini d. Tu Youyou

7 If a mixer or toaster or other such electrical equipment malfunctions and catches fire, which of these can you use to control and extinguish the fire?

a. Vegetable oil b. Baking soda c. Baking powder d. Flour

8 Which international treaty was signed to protect the ozone layer by phasing out the production of numerous substances responsible for ozone depletion?

a. Montreal Protocol b. Kyoti Protocol

c. Paris Agreement d. Glasgow Summit

9 What is the official language of Bhutan?

a. Newari b. Druk c. Dzongkha d. Tibetan

10 Which genre of music was invented in New Orleans, United States in the late 19th and early 20th centuries, and combines African American music with European music?

a. Rap b. Jazz c. Blues d. Chutney

Quiz Yourself 4

Answer these questions.

1 What was the name of the first artificial satellite launched into space in 1957?

a. Explorer b. Laika c. Voyager d. Sputnik

2 Which was the first non-animal mascot of the 2014 Commonwealth Games held in Glasgow?

a. Holly b. Mistletoe c. Thistle d. Moss

3 Which instrument is used to make things that are very distant from us look bigger?

a. Telescope b. Microscope c. Magnifying glass d. Television

4 Which Carnatic music vocalist was the first musician to win the Bharat Ratna, awarded in 1998?

a. Bhupen Hazarika b. Bhimsen Joshi

c. MS Subbulakshmi d. Lata Mangeshkar

5 Which animal, famed for its fur, is Argentina's most endangered animal?

a. Mink b. Sable c. Red fox d. Chinchilla

6 What is J K Rowling's favourite animal?

a. Silver doe b. Otter c. Grim d. Wolf

7 What do we call a person or entity who writes a cheque as payment to another?

a. Payee b. Drawee c. Bearer d. Recipient

8 The World Health Organisation (WHO) first learned of this new virus on 31 December 2019, after news of cases of 'viral pneumonia' in ....

a. Australia b. New Zealand c. China d. India

9 Under which dynasty were the monuments and sculptures of Mahabalipuram built?

a. Chola b. Pallava c. Chera d. Pandya

10 Which famous Indian artist is most known for his painting of the Bindu?

a. Raja Ravi Varma b. MF Husain

c. Amrita Sher-Gil d. SH Raza

Answer Key

Page 9: 1. Bungalow; 2. Cash; 3. Dacoit; 4. Mango; 5. Mahout; 6. Juggernaut; 7. Bangle; 8. Cheetah

F	G	U	R	Y	T	E	R	I	C
E	V	M	B	M	O	D	C	G	H
P	D	A	C	O	I	T	K	G	E
B	U	N	G	A	L	O	W	F	E
J	U	G	G	E	R	N	A	U	T
A	D	O	U	O	R	T	S	E	A
S	C	H	O	L	T	E	A	R	H
M	A	H	O	U	T	U	T	S	H
F	S	Z	E	B	A	N	G	L	E
R	H	E	D	A	C	O	I	T	D

Page 10-11: 1. Indian banyan; 2. Sugi pine; 3. Frangipani; 4. Baobab; 5. Royal oak; 6. Deodar; 7. Willow; 8. Cork oak; 9. Rhododendron; 10. Silver birch; 11. Siberian fir; 12. Silver fern

Page 12-13: 1. Mysore; 2. Thiruvananthapuram; 3. Coimbatore; 4. Visakhapatnam; 5. Hampi; 6. Kozhikode; 7. Hyderabad; 8. Madurai; 9. Tirupati; 10. Bengaluru; 11. Nizamabad; 12. Kochi; 13. Amaravati; 14. Warangal; 15. Thanjavur

Page 14: 1. The Book Thief; 2. Diary of a Wimpy Kid; 3. James and the Giant Peach; 4. Twenty Thousand Leagues Under the Sea; 5. The Jungle Book; 6. Charlotte's Web; 7. The Thousand and One Nights; 8. Aesop's Fables; 9. The Secret Garden; 10. Anne of Green Gables; 11. A Wrinkle in Time; 12. Black Beauty

Page: 15:

V	A	S	D	F	A	E	I	B	T
I	W	A	L	A	M	U	O	A	M
C	E	I	U	A	W	P	Q	I	F
T	A	N	G	A	N	Y	I	K	A
O	X	T	V	D	W	U	J	A	G
R	O	I	R	E	P	U	S	L	L
I	L	O	C	H	N	E	S	S	E
A	K	P	B	J	M	A	G	K	Z

1. Lake Baikal; 2. Lake Tanganyika; 3. Lake Superior; 4. Loch Ness; 5. Lake Victoria; 6. Lake Malawi

Page 16: 1. Hustle; 2. Cinema; 3. Fork; 4. Smog; 5. Tiger; 6. Emoticon; 7. Enormous; 8. Fantastic; 9. Hotel; 10. Internet

Page 17: 1. Rio De Janeiro; 2. Maldives; 3. Kyoto Protocol; 4. Carbon footprint; 5. United Nations; 6. An Inconvenient Truth; 7. Montreal Protocol

Page 18: 1. ☹; 2. ☺; 3. ☺; 4. ☺; 5. ☺; 6. ☹

Page 19: 1. Angel; 2. Bigar Cascade; 3. Rhine; 4. Kaieteur; 5. Gullfoss; 6. Kunchikal; 7. Victoria

Page 20-21: 1. Shinkansen; 2. Mount Fugi; 3. Bento Box; 4. Shogun; 5. Ikebana; 6. Kimono; 7. Sensei; 8. Sushi 9. Shinto; 10. Sumo; 11. Judo; 12. Karate

Page 22-23: 2. Ascend slowly and safely at all times.
3. Check your gear and make sure you know how to use it.
4. Never dive beyond your qualification or your comfort zone.
5. Stay physically fit to increase safety on dives.
6. Plan your dive and dive your plan.
7. Use one-third of your air supply going down, another third during the return and the final third as a safety reserve.
8. Use the buddy system unless you have been properly trained to dive alone.
9. Practise vital skills to avoid injury and accidents.
10. Establish positive buoyancy at the surface. This means you should float easily when you reach the surface.

Page 24: 1. Golden snitch; 2. Keeper; 3. Ferret; 4. Basilisk; 5. Protego; 6. 'Never tickle a sleeping dragon'; 7. The Daily Prophet; 8. Firebolt; 9. Fang; 10. Ministry of Magic, Misuse of Muggle Artefacts Department; 11. The Fat Lady; 12. Nurmengard; 13. Riddle's diary with Harry's sock; 14. Fawkes

Page 25: 1. southernmost; 2. tango; 3. Perito Moreno; 4. Mount Aconcagua; 5. fingerprinting; 6. chinchilla; 7. Lionel Messi; 8. polo

Page 26: Correct sequence: 6, 3, 4, 5, 2, 1

Page 27: 1. e; 2. c; 3. f; 4. h; 5. g; 6. d; 7. a; 8. b

Page 28: 1. Mamallapuram; 2. beach; 3. Coromandel; 4. Pallava; 5. Ganges; 6. chariot; 7. Mahabharata; 8. hill; 9. bull; 10. tsunami

Page 29: 1. Birmingham; 2. Malaysia; 3. thistle; 4. Victoria; 5. Borobi; 6. Australia

Page 30-31: 1. c; Tunisia 2. f; Sweden 3. h; USA 4. e; USA 5. a; India 6. g; India 7. b; USA 8. d; Hong Kong

Page 32-33: Across: 1. Mysore; 3. Pratapgarh 4. Kanyakumari; 7. New Delhi; 8. Port Blair; 9. Namchi
Down: 2. Shravanabelagola; 4. Kolkata; 5. Udaipur; 6. Hyderabad

Page 34-35: 1. Country; 2. Soul; 3. Heavy metal; 4. Gospel; 5. Classical; 6. Folk; 7. Reggae; 8. Hip-hop; 9. Jazz; 10. Pop; 11. Rock

Page 36-37: 1. Land of Thunder Dragon; 2. Dzongkha; 3. archery; 4. tobacco; 5. traffic lights; 6. takin; 7. Buddhism; 8. Jigme Dorji; 9. Tiger's Nest Monastery; 10. Paro; 11. chillies; 12. ankle-length

Page 38-39: 1. China, mountain; 2. Iceland, volcanoes; 3. Norway, National; 4. Africa, Kilimanjaro; 5. Austria, Alps; 6. Pakistan, Kilometres

Page 40-41: 1. sugarcane; 2. cotton; 3. tea; 4. coffee; 5. mustard; 6. coconut; 7. jute; 8. sunflower

Page 42-43:

E	E	K	S	R	E	L	W	O	B
B	R	A	I	L	L	E	L	R	T
D	E	L	Z	S	P	O	E	E	R
E	P	A	Z	T	E	T	O	G	A
Y	M	S	U	R	I	A	P	D	M
P	A	H	C	Z	A	R	R	D	F
P	M	N	A	Z	E	D	D	I	E
U	A	I	J	S	I	R	R	E	F
G	Z	K	S	L	U	M	P	S	W
T	X	O	P	I	L	A	T	E	S
O	E	V	K	L	E	B	E	L	M

1. Braille; 2. Pilates; 3. Kalashnikov; 4. Bowler; 5. Leotard; 6. Jacuzzi; 7. Diesel; 8. Guppy; 9. Ampere; 10. Ferris

Page 44-45: 1. Burj Khalifa; 2. Rose City; 3. Bethlehem; 4. 9000 BCE; 5. Dead Sea; 6. 200,000, Hanging Gardens of Babylon; 7. Suez Canal; 8. Mocha; 9. stylus, clay tablets; 10. Aswan Dam, Nile

Page 46-47: 1. Alexander Fleming; 2. *penicillium notatum*; 3. bacteria; 4. University of Oxford; 5. injections; 6. 20,000 litres; 7. mass producing; 8. 200 times; 9. X-rays, 1%; 10. Nobel Prize for Physiology or Medicine

Page 48: 1. d; 2. f; 3. e; 4. b; 5. h; 6. g; 7. a; 8. c

Page 49:

K	G	P	R	S	I	S	N	G	I	P	R
W	E	Y	N	A	U	K	E	E	L	R	E
A	N	S	W	M	N	A	W	E	T	I	I
M	G	U	H	N	H	N	C	H	M	M	R
E	H	N	A	U	E	D	A	O	U	O	R
N	I	Y	T	J	R	E	N	W	S	Z	E
K	S	K	G	O	E	R	N	E	T	T	F
R	K	T	O	M	T	B	O	V	B	R	N
U	H	S	E	A	H	E	T	E	E	U	A
M	A	E	S	N	A	R	D	R	D	B	H
A	N	N	O	I	T	G	O	I	O	A	O
H	T	C	H	I	L	I	N	H	N	R	J

1. Lee Kuan Yew; 2. Genghis Khan; 3. Sam Nujoma, 4. Johan Ferrier; 5. Skanderbeg; 6. Kwame Nkrumah

Page 50-51: 1. d; 2. c; 3. e; 4. b; 5. a; 6. g; 7. h; 8. i; 9. j; 10. f

Page 52-53: Across: 1. Dibrugarh; 7. Deccan Queen; 8. Zones
Down: 1. Double Decker; 2. Bombay; 3. Ghum; 4. Howrah; 5. Fairy Queen; 6. Varanasi

Page 54: 1. football; 2. boxing; 3. rugby; 4. cricket; 5. tennis; 6. skiing; 7. basketball; 8. golf

Page 55: 1. d, Sansad Bhavan; 2. f, States General; 3. b, Palace of Westmister; 4. c, The United States of Congress; 5. a, The Centre Block; 6. e, The Beehive

Page 56: 1. MC Mary Kom; 2. Gopinath Bordoloi; 3. Danny Denzongpa; 4. Dipa Karmakar; 5. Rani Gaidinliu; 6. Bhupen Hazarika; 7. Bhaichung Bhutia; 8. Indira Goswami

Page 57: 1. Mexico; 2. India; 3. Turkey; 4. Germany; 5. Italy; 6. Argentina; 7. South Africa; 8. France; 9. Australia; 10. Japan 11. The Netherlands; 12. Spain

Page 58-59: 1. iPad; 2. *Twenty Thousand Leagues Under the Sea*; 3. cyberspace; 4. *2001: A Space Odyssey*; 5. bone conduction; 6. video conferencing; 7. USB-type; 8. ASIMO; 9. the moon

Page 60-61: 1. North America and Europe; 2. 10; 3. economic development; 4. welfare; 5. 15; 6. world oil market; 7. Bangladesh, India, Myanmar, Sri Lanka, Thailand, Nepal and Bhutan

Page 62: 1. h; 2. d; 3. f; 4. e; 5. g; 6. a; 7. c; 8. b

Page 63: 1. Bhopal Disaster; 2. marine oil spill; 3. nuclear reactors; 4. 10,000

Page 64-65: 1. K J Yesudas; 2. Begum Akhtar; 3. MS Subbulakshmi; 4. Kumar Gandharva; 5. M Balamuralikrishna; 6. Bhimsen Joshi; 7. M L Vasantha Kumari; 8. Parveen Sultana

Page 66-67: 1. Chemistry; 2. Medicine; 3. Chemistry; 4. Chemistry; 5. Medicine; 6. Medicine; 7. Medicine; 8. Medicine; 9. Medicine; 10. Medicine

Page 68: 1. Dragon's Blood tree; 2. Bats; 3. cowry; 4. bottle tree; 5. skinks; 6. starling; 7. island of bliss

Page 69: 1. Kerala; 2. Andhra Pradesh; 3. Maharashtra; 4. West Bengal; 5. Karnataka; 6. Tamil Nadu

Page 70:

W	T	M	P	O	L	A	R
A	I	P	E	R	T	Y	U
L	I	N	U	I	T	S	S
R	S	L	O	C	S	M	S
U	P	A	V	E	N	A	I
S	P	P	A	L	E	N	A
E	D	F	S	A	H	G	Q
R	A	O	P	N	C	K	E
E	R	W	A	D	I	M	X
X	T	L	R	K	L	L	Z

1. Lapps; 2. Inuit; 3. Iceland, Russia; 4. lichens; 5. Polar; 6. Walrus

Page 71: 1. loan; 2. account; 3. locker; 4. payee; 5. drawee; 6. bearer; 7. interest; 8. fixed; 9. crossed; 10. 3 months; 11. cheque number; 12. EMIs

Page 72: 1. Bangladesh; 2. Bhutan; 3. India; 4. Sri Lanka; 5. Pakistan; 6. Nepal

Page 73: 1. utensils; 2. ketchup; 3. lemon; 4. cookie; 5. cartoon; 6. hamster; 7. shampoo; 8. anonymous

Page 74-75: 1. ii d; 2. iii e; 3. iv b; 4. v a; 5. i c; 6. viii g; 7. vi h; 8. vii f

Page 76-77: 1. Toll; 2. Lane; 3. Agra; 4. Rohtang; 5. Yamuna; 6. Quadrilateral; 7. Leh; 8. Kargil; 9. Ladakh; 10. Jammu; 11. Porbandar; 12. Dras; 13. Corridor; 14. Atal; 15. Silchar; 16. Mumbai; 17. Manali; 18. Taj, Twelve; 19. Syama; 20. Setu; 21. Bharatmala; 22. Mirage;

A	B	T	V	A	Y	O	X	[1]T	H	N	[2]L	M	[3]A	W	T	I
C	O	G	C	J	I	P	[4]R	O	H	T	A	N	G	Y	O	P
D	O	W	E	[5]Y	T	E	K	L	A	E	N	B	R	B	Z	S
Y	J	[6]Q	U	A	D	R	I	L	A	T	E	R	A	[7]L	X	[8]K
G	[9]L	B	C	M	U	W	C	F	B	Q	S	B	J	E	B	A
[10]J	A	M	M	U	X	V	B	S	V	B	F	N	G	H	M	R
B	D	E	B	N	Q	S	[11]P	V	C	V	D	A	[12]D	D	C	G
C	A	H	F	A	L	[13]C	O	R	R	I	D	O	R	D	E	I
O	K	K	D	J	B	Y	R	O	X	P	O	W	[14]A	T	A	L
T	H	B	C	N	H	U	B	K	N	Y	[15]S	H	S	K	G	B
[16]M	B	O	P	L	K	[17]M	A	N	A	L	I	B	L	[18]T	A	J
U	H	I	J	[19]S	L	Z	N	J	G	R	L	V	M	W	D	F
M	R	E	F	Y	J	T	D	H	J	Y	C	I	[20]S	E	T	U
[21]B	H	A	R	A	T	M	A	L	A	H	H	V	L	L	P	K
A	G	F	J	M	N	H	R	H	M	H	A	K	M	V	M	N
I	H	I	U	A	M	H	I	L	[22]M	I	R	A	G	E	U	I

Page 78: 1. Tele, Telephone; 2. Super, Supermarket; 3. Omni, Omnipotent; 4. Super, Superscript; 5. Pre, Preschool; 6. Tele, Telescope; 7. Pre, Precaution

Page 79: 1. b; 2. e; 3. c; 4. a; 5. f; 6. d

Page 80-81: 1. c; 2. b; 3. a; 4. a; 5. b; 6. c; 7. b; 8. a; 9. b

Page 82-83: 1. Humayun's Tomb; 2. Western Ghats; 3. Mahabalipuram; 4. Rajasthan; 5. Elephanta Caves; 6. Keoladeo National Park; 7. Goa; 8. Mountain Railways of India; 9. Jantar Mantar; 10. Mumbai; 11. Ahmadabad; 12. Rani ki Vav in Gujarat

Page 84-85: Across: 2. Telstar; 6. Osumi; 8. Bhaskara; 9. San Marco
Down: 1. Alouette; 3. Explorer; 4. Sputnik; 5. Skylab; 7. Vanguard

Page 86: 1. b; 2. c; 3. a; 4. e; 5. d; 6. h; 7. j; 8. f; 9. g; 10. i

Page 87: 1. b; 2. a; 3. d; 4. e; 5. f; 6. c

Page 88-89: 1. Ukraine; 2. Maastricht; 3. Malta; 4. Belgium; 5. German; 6. Nobel Peace Prize; 7. Finland; 8. United Kingdom; 9. Croatia; 10. Schengen; 11. Norway; 12. Paris

Quiz Yourself 1: 1. b; 2. a; 3. d; 4. b; 5. c; 6. a; 7. d; 8. b; 9. c; 10. a

Quiz Yourself 2: 1. c; 2. a; 3. b; 4. d; 5. b; 6. c; 7. a; 8. d; 9. c; 10. b

Quiz Yourself 3: 1. b; 2. c; 3. a; 4. d; 5. b; 6. d; 7. b; 8. a; 9. c; 10. b

Quiz Yourself 4: 1. d; 2. c; 3. a; 4. c; 5. d; 6. b; 7. a; 8. c; 9. b; 10. d